TITLE P

A Victorian Workhouse

The Lives Of The Paupers

Mildenhall Suffolk

Danny Pearson

COPYRIGHT

www.suffolkhistorybooks.com

ACKNOWLEDGMENTS

Thank you to everyone who foolishly encouraged me to write this book. My sustained suffering, including waking up at 5 am every Saturday and Sunday for two years, has been hard. Now my book is complete, I can sit back and truly thank you for the encouragement.

To the Australian ladies I met on Ancestorian.com, I cannot thank you enough. You were the first people, other than me, to see my work. Thank you for your amazing proofreading, my first ever feedback and reviews. Thank you, Judy, Lesley and Patricia.

Further proofreading was carried out by my sister in law Ruth and my niece Mia- Thank you both.

Massive thanks to Devon Driver of clevereditors.com, you have performed miracles in tidying up my writing. If anyone ever needs any type of editing, without doubt he's your man.

My front cover illustration was created by Paula White, a Suffolk artist. I had originally used a web based service that specialises in book covers, but I was so disappointed with my original cover. It didn't link in any way to Mildenhall or Suffolk. In contrast, Paula has been amazing! She really understood my vision. It was Paula's first illustration since losing her Dad, and her grief had made her worry she may no longer be able to draw. I think we have both greatly benefited from working together. I now have the cover I had always visualised, while Paula has proven she can not only still draw, but has created a stunning piece of work.

Thank you to my wife, Kim. She has supported me in every crazy idea I have ever had, and I've had a lot of them, including this book. Thank you for the hundreds of cups of coffee.

Of course, I have to thank my children Oliver, Samuel and Darcy. You are all equally crazy in very different ways, and you bring to our home a wall of noise and extreme chaos. Writing a book has been almost impossible at times, but I'm not sure the book would have been the same had I written it anywhere else. Thanks for allowing me to share your room—I'm sure it's not ideal to have someone use your playroom as an office.

FOREWORD

It is obvious that Danny Pearson, author, has thoroughly researched the history of Mildenhall Workhouse, and has succeeded in writing a book that shines a light on part of Suffolk's hidden past.

But, instead of being a tedious diary of chronological events, Danny has managed to bring history alive by looking into the lives of certain inmates, and how they did, or did not survive. Sometimes the writing is gory . . . But It's real! This book is a highly readable account and an intriguing but sometimes gruesome chronicle of life during Victorian times in Suffolk.

Charlie Haylock

Suffolk author & historian

PREFACE

My research for this book has enabled me to time travel back to Mildenhall's glorious past. I can now see, hear, and smell Victorian Mildenhall with a perfect image in my head of every street in the town, complete with the characters that once lived here.

As I amble down West street in Mildenhall, Suffolk, I'm met by the local solicitor, Odden Frederic Read, a local celebrity and gentleman of this town. He waves to me from outside his grand Georgian property "The Limes", and holding his cane above his head, he tips his hat towards me. We've come to know each other very well over the previous twelve months, despite our one hundred and thirty year age difference.

I continue on through the town centre to Mill Street, which has been elaborately decorated for the annual Mildenhall flower show, the most anticipated event in the local calendar. Every shop is covered in flowers and bunting, a magnificent effort for just a one day event, and I see old Tin Leg Morley posing outside his shop for a photo. The only traffic I pass is that of a horse and cart, being led by Reginald, the son of the workhouse Master. The sound of the hooves reach me long before the old mare does, and the horse stumbles as she struggles to pull a full cart of fruit and veg. She has a long way to go until she gets to her destination of Brandon.

My tour of this great town takes me past the Cottage Hospital where doctors and nurses sit outside to take in the cool winter air, having earned a well deserved break from running the eight bed hospital. A family also pass by this building, turning down into Fullers Yard. Dressed in rags, the young boy's feet poke through his shoes, but the girl, although of an age where she should be able to walk, is incapable of such a simple task. As she is carried by her mother, she cries in hunger, having only eaten a small amount of bread in the last day, which was gifted to them by the local vicar. The family are seeking shelter before night falls.

It's now dark and the gas lamps have been lit around the town, including outside the Three Kings Public House in St Andrew's Street. As I peer through the bottle green glass window, I can just about make out the animated figure of Charles Docking, his arms and hands waving around, as he persuades two young men who are down on their luck to rob the grave of Johnathon Childerstone. He provides the men with beer until such time they are drunkenly compliant and agree to the morbid plan.

The opening paragraphs to this preface include just some of the characters and true events documented in the following chapters. I hope, like me, you can enjoy travelling back in time to meet more Mildenhall residents as you turn the pages of this book. Join the Facebook page that accompanies this book, "A Victorian Workhouse - The lives of the paupers. Mildenhall Suffolk", where photos and illustrations can be found for every chapter of this book, aiding your imagination as you journey through Victorian Mildenhall.

It's very easy to type "the history of Mildenhall" into any internet search engine, or if you are more traditional, there are many books written on the subject. What you will discover are the landmark events and dates that created this historic market town in Suffolk, and the names of Mildenhall's past celebrities and wealthy families, such as the Hanmers, Norths and Bunburys. You will discover the names of well-known families who all worked hard to build businesses in the town, remembered long after the businesses have gone. Family businesses that served the town so well live on in the memories of local residents, who tell stories and share photos. Both the young and old in the town today will be familiar with names such as the Morleys, Parkers, Stebbings, Maclarens and Snushalls.

What you will not easily discover is how the poorest inhabitants of this great town survived. Who were these poor people, who barely left any evidence of their existence, and how did they find the help they needed? Widowed ladies, orphaned children, the disabled, elderly, and even injured soldiers all struggled in an era with no NHS or old age pension. My research focuses on the Victorian and Edwardian era, a time when "outside relief", what we would call benefits today, was being eliminated due to spiraling costs and a belief that able bodied people were abusing the system.

The early Victorian era was marred with high unemployment and low wages, particularly in the agricultural areas like Suffolk. Outside relief had soared and was not sustainable, so the answer the Victorians found for their problem was to group all the poor of the parishes together in one place where they could feed and clothe them in return for their hard labour. These buildings were known as workhouses, and were effectively prisons for the poor.

This book uncovers the lives of the "paupers" that passed through the doors of Mildenhall's workhouse, which are barely evidenced in the documented history of this town, by taking you on a roller coaster journey through the lives of Mildenhall's poorest Victorian Inhabitants. Through their eyes we see a unique picture of Victorian England, Mildenhall and its surrounding area by uncovering violent crimes, murder, grave robbing, disease, death and sadness. We learn of businesses and buildings that once stood in the town, and buildings that survive today, the history of which we do not appreciate.

I have discovered much through the Mildenhall Museum, a facility we are spoilt to have. It's a wonderful place and if you've never been to visit, or if you haven't been for a few years, you are truly missing out on one of Mildenhall's greatest assets. The Museum holds a handful of surviving records for the Mildenhall Workhouse. Evidence of workhouses is very limited as records have been destroyed and the whole existence of the workhouse system seemingly swept under the carpet. I'm very thankful for the Museum for allowing me access to those records they hold.

I also need to thank the descendants of the families I've researched. Those who I have managed to track down have been very helpful in sharing what they know. Accepting that their ancestors lived in extreme poverty or, in some cases, committed horrendous crimes, is not always an easy thing. We all have a history, and I thank the descendants of all the families I write about for not taking any of my research personally, and for accepting it as a history of those who were let down by a flawed system.

There is a magnificent and supportive community online for family historians, and there are many brilliant Facebook groups full of knowledgeable people. Believe me, you need knowledge and experience to navigate historical records. However, for me the greatest source of help and advice is ancestorian.com—which is a must visit site for any people researching their ancestry.

The research for this book has taken me many months (in fact, years) to put together and it would not have been possible without the support of my wife, Kim. As with most hobbies, they have to exist alongside our busy day to day lives. In order not to inconvenience my family, I set my alarm for 5:00am, or 5:30am if I fancy a lie-in, every Saturday and Sunday, and lock myself away in the study to cram in as much work as possible before the children wake up. The study, distractingly, also doubles as the kids' playroom. Kim would always follow me down, make me coffee, and pretend to be interested in my ramblings about long forgotten individuals of the town. I hope now that I have written about these individuals in context, my ramblings make more sense to her.

BLANK PAGE

CHAPTER ONE

The early Parish Workhouse 1723 – 1834

My work has centred on the lives of Victorian families; however, I'm a firm believer that as with all things in life, you need to know how you got to where you are. I can't wait for this book to take you on a journey through Victorian Mildenhall, but first we must look back at how the Victorian workhouse developed, and why the Victorians used this solution to poverty. With that in mind, we'll begin our journey by looking at Mildenhall's first workhouse.

Workhouses were not a Victorian invention. Although they're closely associated with that particular era, what the Victorians did was take ideas that had existed for 100's of years and stitch them together in the Poor Law Amendment Act of 1834.

Going back centuries (and I'm sure going forward centuries too), there have been questions posed about how we can help the poor. I think everyone agrees that any individual who has fallen on bad times, or can't earn money due to a disability, requires some form of assistance. What's often debated is how to stop able bodied people from claiming assistance in the form of money that they don't deserve? How do you ensure the able bodied are trying to find work and not live off handouts? These are questions you hear posed even today, and they are the exact same questions that led the Victorians down the drastic route to workhouses.

So, we need to travel even further back to find the root of the workhouse. In medieval times, looking after the poor in the parish had always been taken on by religious institutions. They taught the population that it was their Christian duty to help those in poverty, so parishioners paid 10% of their income to the church. Tithe barns were set up where 10% of a landowner's crop would be taken and stored for the Church as well. Amongst other things, the tithe and crops were used to provide relief for the poor.

In 1536 the Church's aid to the poor came to a grinding halt. King Henry VIII, after not being granted an annulment of his marriage to Catherine of Aragon, had one of the largest tantrums in history, which resulted in Henry making himself the supreme head of the Church of England. Henry then carried out the dissolution of the monasteries. Being fed up with the Church's power, he took away the wealth from the religious institutes to increase the income of the Crown, and many of the items taken from monastic properties were sold off to fund Henry VIII's military campaigns.

Mildenhall Church itself suffered in this period, as the stained-glass windows installed in the previous century were removed and smashed, and many of the Mildenhall locals were fined for refusing to accept Protestantism. This was the beginning of many years of turmoil for the Church. In 1651, a man was hired and paid one shilling a day to destroy symbols relating to the Catholic religion. This hired vandal destroyed what remained of the stained-glass windows, as well as defacing angels carved into the roof in the aisles. Fortunately for Mildenhall, the angels in the roof of the nave were high enough to survive the defacing, but do show signs of being shot.

The poor and sick had relied on the church having the wealth to provide "poor relief". Without this aid, poverty was rising and the number of vagabonds was increasing. By the time Elizabeth I came to the throne, it became clear that new legislation was needed to deal with the issue. In 1601, the Act for the Relief of the Poor (sometimes called the "old poor law") made it compulsory for parishes to levy a poor rate on the householders of the parish. The amount a household paid was linked to the value of their property. This tax is still with us today and is now known as Council Tax. Most of the money collected by the 1601 Poor Law was given to those in need in the form of out-relief or "handouts". This aid was only available to individuals who couldn't work, and came in the form of money, clothes, or food. Able bodied people were expected to provide some kind of labour in return for their handout. For example, they could be given materials such as wool or hemp to work on and once the work was complete, they had earned their handout. Another relevant part of the 1601 Act worth noting was the mention of "houses". The "blameless" poor could be housed in Almshouses or poor houses. So, in the 1601 Act we already have the fundamentals of the Victorian workhouse. There was work for the able bodied, and houses for the poor, but they were just not joined together at this stage.

It didn't take long before the Parishes realised the cost saving and potential profit that could be made by housing the poor in one place, rather than paying out relief to many separate individuals. If they brought many of them together under one roof, they could keep one fire going to warm them all, and provide food at a much-reduced cost with less waste. From 1620 onwards, what we would recognise as the first "workhouses" began to appear across the country and "farming the poor" became a recognised way to reduce the parishes' cost of Poor Relief. This involved hiring out the poor as day labourers. This process could be subcontracted out to a third party who made their money by charging the parish a fee, as well as keeping profit from work carried out by the poor they were farming.

In 1662, the Poor Relief Act, or Settlement and Removal Act, became law and the poor were now subject to new settlement and removal laws. These laws enabled parishes to send individuals whom they felt may claim poor relief from them back to the parish of their last settlement. The settlement was the legal parish to which you belonged, and there were a few ways to achieve settlement in a parish. At birth you would have inherited your settlement status from your father, but this could be changed by living in a parish for forty days without a complaint against you. If you were a female you could marry a man from the parish and take his settlement status. Additionally, young men could have a seven year apprenticeship in a parish and live in a house with a rent of at least £10 per year. The Mildenhall Museum has some interesting examples of removal documentation for poor men and women who the parish did not want around the town. Pregnant women without a partner were the group of people the parish were most keen to remove, so they wouldn't become liable for the poor relief of the mother and child. There are even stories of women being moved over parish boundaries just before birth.

In 1697, the shaming of the poor took outrageous steps towards behaviour that simply would not be acceptable today. The 1697 Badging of the Poor Act required anyone claiming poor relief, and their wife and children, to wear either a red or blue cloth on their right shoulder, with the initial of the parish from which they were claiming relief followed by a "P".

It wasn't until 1723 that the workhouse was first mentioned in legislation in the Workhouse Test Act. The workhouse test was intended to reduce the amount of poor claimants, the test being the entering of the house itself. If you entered the workhouse voluntarily then, it was thought, you must be in desperate need of help. It was an idea that would form a key component of the Victorian workhouses.

The 1723 Act provided a framework for parishes to set up these workhouses and formalise practices that were already in existence. Workhouses were now being built or set up in existing buildings at a tremendous rate, and by 1775 there were over 2000 workhouses in the country.

It was during this workhouse boom that Mildenhall set up its first workhouse. After a parish meeting held on 26th February 1723, it was agreed that Sir Thomas Hanmer, Lord of the Manor of Mildenhall and Speaker of the House of Commons, would sell two dwellings situated in the south west corner of the churchyard, which were occupied by James Webb and Francis Dennis. The vicar and several parishioners voluntarily agreed to contribute towards the repair or rebuilding of these dwellings so that they were suitable for housing the poor. The badging of the poor continued until 1810, although an act passed in 1782 meant that "paupers of good character" could leave off the badge.

The building that housed Mildenhall's first workhouse still stands in the corner of the churchyard today and is a Grade II listed private residence. Next door to the workhouse is another building, of medieval origin, that was used to house the Master and Matron of the workhouse along with their family. The doorway to the main building of the old workhouse is surrounded by a 15th century arch of limestone, and above these are two Coats of Arms. One of these Coats of Arms relates to Edward the Confessor and the other to the abbey of St Edmundsbury, suggesting that the early buildings belonged to the abbey. The abbey would have lost ownership of this building after the dissolution of the monasteries.

The ownership of the Mildenhall estate then came into the possession of Edward North, 1st Baron of Kirtling, and remained in the possession of the North family for four generations.. The last North to own the Estate of Mildenhall was Sir Henry North, who tragically shot himself in the manor house leaving no issue. It was then that the estate was inherited by Thomas Hanmer, the nephew of Sir Henry North.

In 1782, legislation was moving closer and closer to creating the workhouse system that would be used in the Victorian era. In the 1782 poor relief act, known as the Thomas Gilbert's Act, parishes were allowed to form unions to share and reduce the cost of poor relief by operating a shared poorhouse. The poorhouses were only for the old, sick and infirm. Able bodied poor were not able to enter as they were still only permitted out-relief, and in turn were found work near to their homes.

Further help came to the poor in 1795 with the Speenhamland system. This was an allowance system that topped up the wages of the poor to a level where they could survive without starvation and extreme poverty, and was, in effect, the first "living wage". The level of allowance awarded to the poor claimant was linked to the price of bread and the number of children in the family. The allowance could go up or down accordingly. The Speenhamland system was easily abused, and allowed farmers to pay their workers lower wages, knowing that the Parish would top them up.

The Poor Relief became a large burden on the parishes as costs soared at the start of the 1800s. This wasn't just caused by the Speenhamland allowance system, but also the end of the Napoleonic wars in 1815. During the Napoleonic wars, Britain increased its Navy from 15,000 sailors to 133,000, and its Army from 40,000 soldiers to 250,000. As the war ended, these British military forces were again reduced in numbers. The returning soldiers and sailors, now unemployed, returned to their parishes looking for work. There wasn't enough work to be found however, resulting in many extra claims on the poor relief system.

Coinciding with the end of the Napoleonic wars was the introduction of the Corn Laws, the first in 1815. This new law restricted and taxed corn imported from outside Britain. Consequently, the Corn Laws made landowners very wealthy and the poor even poorer. At this time, only landowners were allowed to vote, despite making up just 3% of the population, meaning that the Corn Laws were here to stay.

With the increase in Poor Relief claimants together with the increase in the price of bread, the cost of poor relief was rocketing upwards. The ratepayers were increasingly being asked for more money to help the poor of their parish. Between 1795 to 1815, the national poor relief bill had quadrupled from £2 million to £8 million. Ratepayers no longer felt it was their Christian duty to help the poor, and there was a growing feeling that the poor were happy to take a handout without any attempt to work. The ratepayers felt it was all too easy and comfortable for the poor, and that they were the ones footing the bill for the lazy inhabitants of the parish.

By the 1830s the "old poor law" simply was not working. It was too costly, and was in no way encouraging the unemployed to find work. The Government attempted to cut the poor rate but this led to civil unrest amongst the claimants, particularly in rural areas. In 1830, the rural workers of East Anglia and the South rose together and started a campaign of riots known as the Swing Riots. Farming in Britain had changed over recent years, and there was a move away from long term employment towards casual farm hands. Workers were unable to claim poor relief if farmers only employed them for half the year, and if farm labourers did find work, wages were low due to the high availability of labour. Farm labourers were not only being replaced by readily available workers, such as returning soldiers, but also new technology. Machines, such as threshers, were invented at an increasingly fast rate by the Victorians, taking the place of many farm workers.

East Anglia was a particular hot bed for the Swing Riots, as the county pioneered these new farming methods. Threshing machines were now common across all towns in Suffolk, and agricultural labouring in Suffolk had been totally transformed into short contract work. Rioters assembled en masse in rural towns to demand higher wages, and these riots were certainly not peaceful marches. Gangs of poor agricultural labourers arrived in towns, intending to cause mass chaos by destroying farm machinery, tithe barns, and workhouses—

all of which were symbols they associated with their oppression.

Punishment was severe for those found guilty of taking part in the riots. Although over 800 men were acquitted, over 700 others were deported, another 644 imprisoned, and 252 sentenced to death. Like many working-class families in East Anglia, my relatives in the 1830s were agricultural workers. I wonder how the Swing Riots affected my Flack ancestors labouring on farms in Lakenheath, and the Pearsons who were providing farm labour around Great Whelnetham near Bury St. Edmunds. No doubt they were severely affected by the low wages, and most probably would have been involved in or impacted by the riots to some degree.

Landowners and ratepayers became worried and unnerved by the events in the 1830s and in 1832 a Royal Commission was set up to report on the problems and civil unrest England was experiencing. The Royal Commission's report was completed in 1834, and its conclusions led to what would become the 1834 Poor Law Amendment Act. The Swing Rioters had managed to change the way Britain would deal with the poor, but the saying "Be careful what you wish for" could be applied now.

The 1834 Poor Law Amendment Act didn't contain many new ideas, rather it incorporated and joined several legislations from previous years. The intention was for this new poor relief to only be applied for by the truly desperate, being a last act of desperation that would come with as much stigma as it did relief.

The houses were to be unwelcoming and intimidating, with families split and segregated on arrival. The work was also hard and long, particularly for the men, who would be given tasks such as stone breaking, corn grinding and bone crushing. The female inmates would carry out the domestic duties required to keep the workhouse running, such as cleaning, sewing, scrubbing, kitchen work and making uniforms. Those who were more elderly or infirm could be given jobs such as oakum picking

Bone crushing work was removed from the workhouses in 1845, when inmates at the Andover Workhouse in Hampshire were found to be fighting over the bones, so they could eat the marrow and gristle that was still attached. The bones were intended to be crushed in the workhouse to produce fertiliser and were often putrid and definitely not fit for human consumption. This scandal was reported nationwide and demonstrated just how tough the conditions could be in these newly formed union workhouses.

Oakum picking was a job that could be given to those inmates less mobile, elderly or infirm. It was still tedious however, and hard on the fingers and thumbs. It consisted of picking apart old rope, to reduce it back down to single fibers, so that it could be mixed with tar and used as caulking in ship repairs.

Stone breaking was a favourite job to be given to the vagrants. Large rocks and stones were supplied to the inmates to be broken down into small stones that could then be used for road making. The stones needed to pass through a grid to ensure the grading was correct. In 1870, Henry Saxon Snell, who would go on to design a workhouse for Mildenhall that was never built, designed a work cell for stone breaking that had a grid on the window so that the broken up smaller stones could be pushed through for grading. The window could be opened from the outside so that large rocks could be placed into the room, ready for the inmate to start work. These cells had sleeping areas so that vagrants could also be housed in these rooms. Once the stones had all been pushed back through the grid, they had done their work and earned their accommodation. They were then free to move on to their next stop, normally another workhouse, further along their tramping route.

The 1834 Poor Law built on the idea of the Gilbert Act of placing parishes together as a Union, with a board of Guardians representing the parishes of the union who administered the Poor Law. The workhouse of the 1834 Act became a "deterrent workhouse". Out-relief was severely restricted and, for the first time, the able-bodied poor needed to enter the workhouse if they were to claim poor relief. The 1834 act was based on the 1723 idea of the "workhouse test". The idea was that conditions inside the workhouse would be more miserable than the conditions of a working pauper outside, the "test" being the entering of the workhouse despite knowing the conditions inside.

Many unions constructed purpose-built workhouses between 1835 and 1840 to ensure they could administer the new Poor Law and have enough capacity for inmates throughout the union. Mildenhall, for the time being, continued with the existing parish workhouse, which now became the Union Workhouse.

CHAPTER TWO

The Mildenhall Union Workhouse

We now understand how the changes in the poor relief system eventually led to the erection of the first Mildenhall Parish Workhouse, and how it then transitioned into the Union Workhouse in 1834. This chapter will look at the early years of the Union Workhouse as well as the "workhouse test," which was the actual act of entering the workhouse. What was like for the poor of the Mildenhall Union who walked through the workhouse door? Understanding the Victorian workhouse will help with your time travelling experience in the following chapters, when we meet some of the Victorian inhabitants of Mildenhall.

In 1834, counties were still divided up into smaller administrative divisions called hundreds. Mildenhall was part of the Lackford Hundred, which consisted of 17 different parishes, including Newmarket, Worlington, Lakenheath, Thetford and Barton Mills. As poor unions formed across the country, it was still not known what the union would look like for the Lackford Hundred. Would the parishes from the hundred form one union, or join parishes from neighbouring hundreds? Mildenhall and the rest of the Lackford Hundred would have to wait another year until this question was finally answered.

In 1835, Dr James Kay (later to be known as Sir James Kay Shuttleworth), who was a well known British politician of the time, was appointed the Poor Law Commissioner for Suffolk and Norfolk.

On October 1st 1835, Dr James Kay visited the Lackford Hundred to hold a meeting. In attendance were Lord William Powlett, Lord of the Manor of Santon Downham; William Henry Fitzroy, Earl of Euston, which is a small village near Thetford; Sir Henry Bunbury, Lord of the Manor of Mildenhall; as well as eight other magistrates. Together they discussed the union of the Lackford Hundred. They voted unanimously in favour of a Union Workhouse in Mildenhall, although Lord William Powlett requested that Brandon not be included in this particular union.

Following the meeting, Dr James Kay wrote to the central board submitting the plan for the Mildenhall Union workhouse. As part of this plan, the old Mildenhall parish workhouse would be enlarged to accommodate 100 inmates. In his letter, Dr James Kay described the area as an "unpeopled Hundred" and went on to call it "one immense rabbit warren inhabited by a few poachers and a few more paupers". The population of the district was just 7,500 but it was decided not to include any other parishes in the Union. The alterations were approved on 12th December 1835, and carried out at a cost of £400.

The Board of Guardians was elected and Dr James Kay met with the new members on 13th November 1835 to introduce them to the new regulations. It was agreed that alterations were needed to the old workhouse to ensure "correct classification of inmates and provide maintenance of discipline", as this was all part of the new Act to deter the poor from entering the workhouse and claiming relief.

The Mildenhall Workhouse was now functioning as the Union Workhouse, so insurance was taken out on the building in February 1836. The content of the insurance document gives us some idea of how the adjoining buildings (which no longer exist) might have looked. The main building, described as "brick and tile", was insured for £450, an "outhouse and porters lodge (wood and tile) adjoining near" was insured for £25 and a wash house at the bottom of the yard was insured for £25, making a total insured sum of £500.

The supply of provisions was put out to tender for local tradesmen. The successful tenders and suppliers to the workhouse were Mr. Mills for meat and suet, Mr. Pettit for bread, Mr. Large for butter and cheese and Mr. Owers for malt and hops.

The workhouses had previously been heavily criticised for providing meals that might have encouraged paupers to enter the workhouse. In the post-1834 workhouse, this would certainly not be the case, as meals were now intentionally monotonous, bland and eaten in silence. Disorderly behaviour could also be punished by a change of diet, in addition to confinement. The Workhouses had previously been heavily criticised for providing meals that might have encouraged paupers to enter the workhouse, but in the post-1834 workhouse this would certainly not be the case. As part of the "test", unions could select a very basic meal plan from 6 different dietary tables laid out by the Poor Law Commissioners..

Bread was the staple food and made up the bulk of each meal. The bread at breakfast was served with gruel or porridge, both being made of oatmeal and water. The inmates had more variety when it came to lunch and three days a week they were given meat for this midday meal, which were usually cheap cuts of beef or mutton. When it came to supper time, the inmates were given either bread and cheese, or bread and broth.

These bland meals were often created in unsanitary conditions. Hygiene in the workhouses was not a consideration. There exist accounts of visitors to workhouses who witnessed and reported that old people were picking rat faeces out of their oatmeal and black beetles were being found in the food.

The Mildenhall Union was now fully functional and any pauper who applied for poor relief would now find themselves having to enter the Union Workhouse. Entering the workhouse was a seriously distressing ordeal and was cruelly intended to be so. Paupers, already in a desperate and destitute situation, would now endure a stressful formal interview with the relieving officer before being allowed entry to the workhouse. Once a new workhouse inmate had passed through the porter lodge, they were examined by a medical officer before being stripped and washed, and issued the standard workhouse uniform. The inmates' own clothing that they wore on entry was taken away to be washed and stored, ready for a time when the pauper would be discharged from the workhouse.

The workhouse uniform was another form of control over the oppressed inmates. They were unable to leave the workhouse wearing the uniform without prior permission. If they did this, it would be treated as theft from the Union, and was punishable by prison and hard labour. In the archived local newspapers from the time, there are many reports of inmates being given prison sentences for stealing or destroying workhouse clothes from the Mildenhall Union.

Families were required to enter and leave the workhouse together. A husband could not place his children or wife in a workhouse while he continued to work on the outside, as this would be seen as abandoning your family at the expense of the ratepayers. Entering the workhouse was a scary and unnecessarily evil ordeal, but worse was to come for families. Once inside, husbands, wives and children were all separated and could be punished if they attempted to talk to each other. There existed separate areas for different classification of inmates. Males, females, girls, boys, old and infirm all had their own areas within the workhouse, and the interiors and exteriors of workhouses were designed so that each class of inmate would not come into contact with each other.

The separation of children from their parents is to me by far the saddest and most upsetting detail of the Victorian workhouse. Young children who were living in extreme poverty, often weak and sick, were taken away from their parents at the time they needed them most. The children would be moved to a room full of strangers, unless they were lucky enough to have a sibling of the same sex to comfort them.

Children under seven were allowed to stay in the female ward, but only if the Board of Guardians felt it was acceptable. Each case had to be considered on its own merits. Parents were allowed to visit their children for a limited period at the discretion of the Board of Guardians, this visit being referred to as an "interview" and often taking place on a Sunday.

I find it hard to believe this segregation of families wouldn't have impacted the mental well-being of both the parents and children. The need to embrace and comfort their poor children must have been immense. The famous actor, Charlie Chaplin, spent time in Lambeth Workhouse, and in his autobiography, he spoke of the sadness his mother felt at being separated from her children. Charlie Chaplin recalls a time when he and his half-brother returned to the workhouse after having been sent to a school for the day, and he was met at the gate by his mother, Hannah, dressed in her own clothes. Desperate to see them again, she had discharged herself and the children. They spent the day together playing in Kennington Park and visiting a coffee shop. After this valuable time together, she re-admitted them all to the workhouse.

The workhouses and the lives of those who entered them have almost been erased from history. Very few records exist from the workhouses, and those records that are available often only tell the side of the story of those responsible for the administration of the poor law.

In the following chapters, we will meet some individuals who lived through the horror of the workhouse in Mildenhall. They are real life stories that have been pieced together through fragments and clues left behind. These clues will shed light on the shadowy past of the town, when the poor were viewed as criminals just for the fact of being poor.

CHAPTER THREE

The Jessups Master & Matron of the Workhouse

Charles Augustus Jessup, also known as (C. A. Jessup) was a strict but fair man, and his wife Sarah Jane (Jeanie to friends), was his able assistant and enforcer of rules. The couple demanded respect and discipline from their inmates in the workhouse, and their twelve rules were found hung in every room and read aloud on the first Monday of every month. In fact, this very action of monthly rule reading was **"Rule number 12"**!

Ruling with an iron fist was skillfully blended with being compassionate and supporting of the poor, the widowed, abandoned and orphaned of the town. **"Rule Number 7"** read, *"The Master and Matron be strictly attentive to the wants and infirmities of the poor both young and old, instructing the former and comforting the latter"*. Charles was a man experienced with strict routines. Being no stranger to the inside of a prison cell, he was a determined and tenacious man, a rule maker and breaker. His life was bookended by trouble and his criminal trials.

Charles and Sarah Jane Jessup gave the Mildenhall Workhouse seventy-three years of service between them. They were a husband and wife team who arrived in Mildenhall as strangers (Furreners, as the locals would have called them in true Suffolk dialect), but soon became recognised faces in the community and an important cog in the workings of Mildenhall life.

These popular custodians of the workhouse first arrived at the old Parish Workhouse, which was set peacefully in the corner of the

Church yard in 1879, having successfully applied for the positions of Master and Matron following an advertisement placed in the Bury Free Press by the Board of Guardians on Saturday, 31st of May, 1879.

Mildenhall Union
Master, Matron and Female Nurse Wanted

The Guardians of the above Union, will at their Meeting to be held at the Board-room of the Union Workhouse on FRIDAY, the 6th day of June, 1879 at Half Past 10 o'clock in the Forenoon, be prepared to Elect a Master, Matron and Nurse for the Union Workhouse. The Candidates must be Man and Wife without incumbrance.

The Master must be fully competent to keep the Books and Accounts and perform all the duties required of him by the Regulations of the Local Government Board and the Guardians, and to manage and superintend the discipline and employment of the Paupers in the Workhouse, and to enter into a Bond in the sum of £100, with two sureties, for the due and faithful discharge of the duties of his office.

The Matron must be able to superintend all the Domestic arrangements of the Workhouse and the Employment of the Female Paupers.

Candidates for the Appointment of Nurse must be respectable single Women or Widows, without incumbrance, between 30 and 50.

The person appointed must make herself generally useful under the direction of the Board of Guardians and the Matron of the Workhouse.

The Salary of the Master will be £40, that of the Matron £20 and that of the Nurse £18 per year, together with Rations and Apartments in the Workhouse.

Applications in the handwriting of the Candidates stating their ages, present employment, and when they will be prepared to enter upon the duties of the respective offices, and accompanied by not more than Six Testimonials of recent date as to character and fitness, to be sent to my Office on or before WEDNESDAY, the 4th of June next. Selected Candidates will have notice to attend the Board, and a reasonable sum for travelling expenses will be paid to the Candidates so attending who are unsuccessful.

By order of the board
GEORGE ISAACSON
Mildenhall, Suffolk, 19th May, 1879, Clerk

Charles Jessup immediately immersed himself into local life, becoming a member of many of the local clubs and committees in Mildenhall, including the early days of the Cricket Club and the Football Club. In 1880, he played in the town's first ever football matches before, in his later years, becoming a referee. In one of these first historic matches for Mildenhall, Charles travelled with the Mildenhall team to play Bury St Edmunds, the scheduled kick off time being 2:30pm. The Bury team, dressed in their shirts, flannel trousers and strong boots, with nearly every man sporting a rather fashionable mustache, were already out on the pitch. Their manager, tapping the glass on his fob watch, waited impatiently for the Mildenhall boys to appear. "Here come the Hall!"—Mildenhall arrived forty-five minutes after kick off with only nine men. As soon as Mildenhall had convinced two passers-by to play for them, the game commenced. The match finished 1-0 to Bury, which was reported in the paper as one goal to love. These truly were the early days of organised football.

Charles Jessup was also a private in the Volunteer Rifles Brigade, where he was highlighted as being the best shot in the 5th Battalion. He was also a consistent winner in local flower shows as he won numerous prizes for his entries, specialising in large blooming Japanese chrysanthemums. If there was an event happening in Mildenhall, then Charles Jessup was likely to be involved.

Charles Jessup first met his wife Sarah Jane while working for the Dorchester Poor Union, where he held the position of "porter of the workhouse". The porter was an important role within the workhouse staff, with a high level of responsibility. They were the front line of security. A Victorian style "bouncer", the porter would prevent unauthorised people from entering the gate, keep a book of anyone who did step inside, examine all parcels for banned substances, search male paupers (female paupers being searched by the Matron) entering or leaving through the gate, ensure articles were not removed from the workhouse, lock all doors and windows at 9:00 pm and take the keys to the Master before collecting the keys again at 6.00 am. He was also expected to help the Master and Matron enforce obedience and subordination.

It took a certain individual and a unique skill set to fulfill the role of porter. He would need to have an air of authority, an intimidating stature and ability to follow a strict routine. Charles Jessup had these in abundance and he was a man who was respected, listened to and followed. Charles was a leader of men who ensured either the rules or the consequences were enforced.

Charles had the required skill set in his DNA. Born in Chichester, Sussex, in 1855, he was the first-born child of four siblings. His parents were Joseph Jessup, school master of the All Saints National School in Islington, and school teacher Charlotte Jessup.

In 1860, Charles was just six years old when tragedy struck his family, his father Joseph dying at just 27 years of age. At the time of his death, Charles' mother was eight months pregnant with Charles's younger sister, Alice, who would also go on to work at Mildenhall Workhouse. When Joseph Jessup left this world, his young wife was left totally unable to care for Charles and his brothers, Edwin and Augustus as well as the unborn Alice.

Life from then on was not easy for the Jessup family. Before Joseph's death, the Jessups had lived comfortably, even affording a domestic servant to help with the chores. By the time of the 1871 census, this had very much changed. In the Victorian era, it was very common for a widow to remarry unbelievably soon after the death of the husband. For a widow, to survive financially on her own was hard in the Victorian era, but Charlotte did not remarry and her wage alone was not enough to support the Jessups, so the family unit was split to survive. Charles' mother, Charlotte, was now the school mistress at Horsham Workhouse, a job that conveniently also provided accommodation for her and Alice, Charles' now nine year old sister.

Charles' brother, Edwin, had been placed in the British Orphan Asylum in Slough. This was an orphanage, like many others, that only took children elected by governors and subscribers of the charity. After losing his father, Edwin would have been a suitable candidate for entry to the orphanage, but only if it was evidently clear that his mother could not provide for him. Edwin's admission to the British Orphan Asylum demonstrates the struggle Charlotte faced trying to provide for her three remaining children by herself.

Throughout his working life, Charles Jessup was employed by three different poor unions, witnessing humans at their lowest ebb, and surrounded by sadness and the deaths of many. He was in charge of men, women and children who were discarded and hidden by Victorian society for being too poor. Witnessing the death of many of these poor individuals was sadly an inescapable part of life in the workhouse. Even before his working life, as a young eight-year-old Charles Jessup seemed unable to escape the harsh reality of human mortality, enduring yet more heartache when his younger brother, Augustus, died, less than two years after the death of his father.

Charles Augustus Jessup was born and christened as Joseph Charles Jessup. Having been named after his father, he went by his given name of Joseph until his early twenties. The catalyst for his name change was an event that occurred in 1873. With the splitting of his family, a teenage Joseph (Charles Jessup) needed shelter and employment. He found both when he was employed as a jeweller's assistant in Marylebone. His employer and shop owner, Mr Bolton Kneller Smart, allowed the young man to live with him and his family in the house adjoining the shop.

Charles Jessup had been working for Mr Smart for two years when there was a robbery in the shop—a daring heist of £1000 of jewellery. The equivalent value today would be about £120,000. On entering the shop one Monday morning, Mr Smart noticed an empty case and, placing his monocle into his round face, he inspected closely. It had been carefully cut open, and the precious jewellery it had stored was missing. Charles Jessup had not been at work that Monday morning, as he had requested both the Sunday and Monday away from work, with the excuse being that he had arranged to go away for a couple of days.

The detective sergeant arrived at the store and on investigation found that the case had been cut by someone who must have had the key to open it first. Mr Smart found this very peculiar as the key to this case had been lost a few months previously, and had still not materialised. Later that day, Charles Jessup arrived back from his two day break and was asked if he had heard anything of the robbery, to which he simply responded "I had not".

With Charles having conveniently been away, and knowing that he would have had the opportunity to take the key used for the robbery, he was searched. The key was found in his possession. At this point Charles could confess to his crime or make up an elaborate story. He opted for the latter, "Two men who I did not know had made me do it".

A warrant was obtained to search the house of Charlotte, Charles' mother. The police dug around his mother's house and found the jewellery buried amongst a crop of trees. Charles had, in fact, not gone away that Sunday night on the eve of the robbery. Instead he carried out his criminal master plan:

1. Conceal himself in the cellar,
2. Gain access to the shop,
3. Steal a large amount of shiny gold things, using a key that everyone knows is missing,
4. Bury stolen property at mum's house,
5. Return to the shop and pretend to know nothing,
6. (Back up plan) Strange men made me do it.

Charles Jessup arrived at court and confessed to the crime, but not before an outrageous excuse was given. He had recently been reading a number of sensational novels about highwaymen and other desperate characters. He had planned to use his acquired wealth to travel abroad and amass even greater wealth, then return to his native country and return all the owed money to his master, plus interest for the time he had been deprived of it. His defence fell on deaf ears and he was sentenced to 18 months hard labour.

On leaving prison Charles Jessup, (still using his real name Joseph at this stage) moved to Dorchester, where he was employed as the Porter of the workhouse. Charles met his future wife, Sarah Jane, at this workhouse. It was the beginning of a career and partnership that would rapidly see them become Master and Matron of the Mildenhall Workhouse.

Sarah Jane had started working at the Dorchester Workhouse as the school mistress in 1874 after the death of her first husband, George Voss . A schoolmistress at a workhouse had a slightly more involved role in the children's lives than that of a standard school teacher. Sarah Jane was much more like a Mary Poppins type character, educating the children for at least three hours a day, which included industrial and moral training, and accompanying the children when they left the premises for exercise or worship. She also kept the children clean and tidy and ensured they maintained good behavior.

Sarah Jane, known to the family as Jeanie, was the first-born child to John and Susan Dean in Dorchester in 1847. Sarah's father, John Dean, was a master tailor for the British army and had a shop at the barracks of the "Dorchester Militia" regiment. Tailoring was a family trade that Sarah's grandfather and grandmother had also listed as their occupations, a skill passed down through the generations that would be more than useful for Sarah in her career in the workhouses. Sarah had eight brothers and sisters in total, two of which died in childhood, her brother Walter at just two years old and her sister Susan at the age of six.

The childhood mortality rate was very high in the Victorian era. In 1850, when Sarah was three years old, the infant mortality rate was around 100 to 200 deaths per 1000. A child born in this era had just a 60% chance of making it to their sixtieth birthday, an age that Sarah herself just managed to surpass by six years.

The high child mortality rate in Victorian England was largely due to causes which today we have under control. Smallpox, measles, whooping cough, diphtheria, dysentery, tuberculosis, scarlet fever as well as poor nutrition and ever-increasing industrial pollution all contributed significantly to the child mortality rate.

Although childhood death was a far more common occurrence in Victorian England than it is now, it was a no less harrowing and heartbreaking experience. At a time when pain management was very limited, parents could do little more than try their best to comfort their distressed child as diseases ripped through their household. Contemporary writers such as Charles Dickens and Charles Darwin documented the loss of their own children, and from these writings it's clear the loss of a child was just as devastating as it is today, despite the more common occurrence.

Medical advancement was still lacking in Victorian England, but visual technology was sweeping ahead. In the mid-1800s, photography was becoming increasingly popular and affordable. The combination of a high child mortality rate, combined with the advancement of the camera, resulted in a genre of photography called "Memento Mori" which today seems bizarre, morbid and utterly fascinating.

Memento Mori photography was the practice of taking memento photos of the deceased. In an era when not many photos were taken, the photo of a deceased family member was often the only photo a family had to remember their recently deceased loved ones. It became common in Victorian England to dress a departed family member, often a child, in a smart or best dress before posing them with the rest of the family for a portrait, Often this was done by propping the departed up on a chair. Due to the long exposure times required by Victorian cameras, the deceased family member can be picked out by their hauntingly clear and sharp features, the result of total stillness during the long exposure time, and juxtaposed by the blurred faces of the living, whose smallest movement resulted in a slightly out of focus face. It is more than possible that Sarah Jane would have been dressed in her best clothes, along with her deceased brother and sister, to have their family photo taken.

In 1873, Sarah married her first husband, George Voss, whose death made her a widow just one year later. George died of the dreaded Victorian disease consumption, which is now known as tuberculosis. George was just one of four million people who died of consumption between 1851 and 1910. The disease would claim its victim over a prolonged period of time, often over a three year period, "consuming" the body and leaving the diseased victim frail, weak and highly contagious. George would have likely known he had tuberculosis when he and Sarah were married.

Consumption was a terribly efficient killer that was strangely romanticised by the Victorian public, with symptoms of the disease mirrored in Victorian fashion. Victims of consumption became pale and thin, which was seen as desirable. Victorian women copied this look by powdering their faces with white powder and wearing bone crushingly tight corsets to give a similar appearance to those suffering. Writers of the era would romanticise the disease as if it were a beautiful way to die. The reality was not so, but perhaps it was the Victorians' way of accepting a disease they couldn't control.

Edgar Allan Poe described his wife as being *'delicately, morbidly angelic'* as she lay dying of consumption.

Emily Brontë described the diseased heroine in Wuthering Heights as, *"rather thin, but young and fresh-complexioned and her eyes sparkled like diamonds"*. Brontë herself would go on to die of consumption, along with her brother and two sisters. Sadly, the reality of dying from consumption was far more horrifying than beautiful.

Sarah was very caring and diligent in her duties as a school mistress. Several articles in the local paper mentioned activities she had arranged for the children of Dorchester Workhouse. She helped organise a Christmas day party in 1876, with the local paper mentioning that Sarah had been, *"assiduous in her attention"*, *"The dining room was adorned with inscriptions "welcome"*, *"A merry Christmas"*, *"Thanks to the Guardians"*, *"Glory to God in the highest"*, *"Peace and Happiness" as well as "VR" and a crown"*. The inmates then had roast beef and plum pudding followed by beer for the adults, snuff and tobacco for the elders, and oranges and fruit for the children.

The strict, ambitious and sometimes foolish Charles, and the caring, devoted, Mary Poppins-esque Sarah began their journey through life together almost immediately after Charles began working in Dorchester. Their opposite natures furnished the couple with all the skills they required for their career. It wasn't long before the two found themselves in Mildenhall.

In 1878 the couple married and Sarah fell pregnant the same year. The couple had a busy twelve months following the pregnancy and marriage. The Jessups added even more excitement into their lives l in August that same year as, led by the ambitious Charles, they handed in their resignations at the Dorchester Workhouse.

Charles and the pregnant Sarah had applied for the Assistant Master and Matron roles at the Southampton Workhouse, sixty miles along the coast from Dorchester. The Jessups were successfully chosen for the roles out of the fourteen applicants. These were roles not normally considered for couples with a family, so I suspect the Board of Guardians appointing them did not know of Sarah's pregnancy. It was not the only information of which the Board of Guardians were unaware, as Charles Jessup had applied for the role under the name "Charles Augustus Jessup," creating his alias from his own middle name followed by the Christian name of his deceased younger brother. This was the first time Charles had used this name, a name by which he would be known for the rest of his life. This new identity helped Charles hide his criminal record for his poorly planned heist, a crime that surely would have seen him rejected for this responsible role.

Obviously, it is not easy to hide a pregnancy, and even harder to hide a baby, so the Board of Guardians would soon discover Sarah was pregnant. The couple's first son was born later that year in the Southampton Workhouse, the couple again commemorating Charles Jessup's deceased brother by naming their son Augustus Charles

Jessup.

The Assistant Master and Matron roles were a huge step up for the Jessups but the ambitious couple would not settle there for long. Possibly due to tension caused by the birth of their son as well as Charles' burning ambitions, they would leave after less than a year into their tenure. In 1879 they handed in their resignations and Mildenhall was about to meet the Jessups! The Jessup family arrived in Suffolk with their eight month old son, Augustus. The Mildenhall Board of Guardians had found their new Master and Matron but neither side could have imagined just how successful an appointment it would become.

In just twelve months, the Jessups had married, moved to Southampton, become Assistant Master and Matron, had their first child, moved to Mildenhall and become Master and Matron of the workhouse. Not only does this show unbelievable dedication to succeeding in life, but it also demonstrates that the Jessups must have been both articulate and impressive in their interviews. To go from porter and schoolmistress to Master and Matron in such a short period of time, whilst caring for a newborn baby, is no small feat. The Mildenhall Board of Guardians had found a very capable couple to run the Union Workhouse.

It didn't take long for Sarah and Charles Jessup to settle into local life after arriving in Mildenhall, and with baby Augustus in tow they made the town their home. The couple had been living in the old churchyard workhouse for a year before Sarah gave birth to their second child, a baby girl named Charlotte, affectionately shortened to Lottie, and named after Charles' mother. Isabel was born a year later, a little sister for Lottie. The Jessup family continued to grow over the next decade, with five more Jessup children born before 1890. Maude, Alice and Florence were followed by Alfred and Reginald. Charles and Sarah had eight children who were all born in the old workhouse building. They experienced the heartbreak of losing a child when baby Alice passed away when she was less than a year old. This left the Jessups as a family of nine, living together in the Master's accommodation part of the old Parish Workhouse. Just as much as the old workhouse was becoming increasingly unfit for the number of paupers in the Mildenhall Union, the Master's accommodation was also now full with the Jessup family of nine.

CHAPTER FOUR

The New Workhouse

The old Parish Workhouse stood peacefully in a quiet corner of Mildenhall, the silence of the churchyard broken only by the sound of the church bells. The workhouse had housed the poor for the last fifty years, but when it came to the attention of the Government they were unimpressed by its beautiful architecture and surroundings, and deemed it unfit for purpose. The Mildenhall Union found itself at crisis point.

The Poor Law Commissioners were very critical of any former parish workhouses and generally insisted that they be replaced. In 1835, right at the outset of the new Poor Law, the Commissioners had issued a series of template designs. As attractive as it may have been, the Mildenhall building did not conform to the Commissioners' vision of a workhouse building, so pressure was heavily applied to the Mildenhall Board of Guardians to create a large building fit for purpose.

Mr . Lockwood, one of Her Majesty's Poor Law inspectors, had been sent to the town by the local government board to preside over a meeting with the Mildenhall Board of Guardians. The meeting to be held at the Bunbury rooms (a boys' school room at the time), would discuss the serious threat that the Mildenhall Union must be dissolved.

Mr. Lockwood opened the meeting by reading a letter from the local government board:

"It appears expedient to the Local Government Board for the better administration of relief to dissolve the Mildenhall Union, and that said board in pursuance of the divided parishes act 1876, have directed Mr Lockwood Esq,. one of their inspectors to hold a local inquiry with respect to the proposal that the said union should be dissolved"

The inspector said that the Local Government Board and Board of Guardians had long been at issue concerning the subject of the Mildenhall Workhouse. He went on to say that, following a report from the Commissioners in Lunacy and the Poor Law inspectors, the Local Government Board had concluded that a new workhouse would be necessary, and unless it was started by 1886 they must dissolve the union.

Several inspections over the last fifty years had resulted in reports that the house was insufficient for the number of inmates housed and unsuitable to meet the requirements of the new Poor Law. As a result, the government was now flexing its muscle to enforce a new workhouse.

The Rev. R. Gwilt, chairman of the Board of Guardians at that time, was nominated to state the views of the guardians. *"The Board of Guardians had given the proposal serious consideration [and] were unwilling to incur the cost of a new building. Britain was in the middle of an agricultural crisis and it was not a suitable time to take on such an expense. The Board of Guardians are not only unwilling to build a new workhouse but are opposed to the dissolution of the union and would protest against extinction."*

If the Mildenhall Union was dissolved then the poor of the district would be required to enter other Union Workhouses such as Newmarket, Thetford and Thingoe (pronounced Thing-hoe which is now part of St Edmundsbury district). The Board of Guardians stated, *"it would not be possible to transport the poor 20 miles to these workhouses particularly those from the fen areas".*

The Board of Guardians proposed that, rather than erect a new building which would cost £7,000 or more, the current workhouse be updated at a cost of £200 to £300.

Sir Charles James Fox Bunbury, Lord of the Manor of Mildenhall, also weighed in with his thoughts. He sent a representative along to the meeting with a letter he had written to be read to the attendees, his thoughts echoing that of the Guardians that, *"the poor could not be expected to travel long distances to Thetford or Newmarket and a compromise must be found to save the Mildenhall Union"*. This support from an influential and powerful figure was still not enough to convince the stubborn Government.

At a time when the children of families living on the fens had to take a boat to school, there was no way the poor of these communities could be expected to travel even further to receive poor relief. To prevent their extinction as a Union, and to continue to provide a workhouse for the poorer members of the Mildenhall parish, the Guardians had to admit defeat and start looking for land to build a new workhouse. A new workhouse was not wanted and would not be welcomed by the people of Mildenhall.

In 1885 the Mildenhall Union Board of Guardians purchased a meadow at the bottom of St Andrews Street (possibly where the bus shelter now sits) with the intention of building the new workhouse on this site. Henry Saxon Snell, an architect who specialised in health facilities, designed the new workhouse that would sit on this land.

Henry Saxon Snell's design split the workhouse over 4 blocks that sat parallel to each other. There was a central corridor that ran from the first block all the way to the last block, linking them all together. This "pavilion block" design was how pretty much all workhouses had been designed from 1870 onwards. It allowed segregation of the inmates into different categories and allowed ventilation of the buildings, which some of the earlier union workhouses had struggled with.

The proposed workhouse was a colossal site, and if built it would be the largest building Mildenhall had ever seen. The current workhouse was an old medieval building, tucked away neatly behind the towering Church which dominated the landscape around Mildenhall. This new superstructure was going to impose itself right on the edge of the town centre, fighting for dominance opposite the church. The locals were not willing to accept the change. One thing I have learnt is throughout history, and still to this day, locals do not like shiny new buildings being built in their town.

In April 1886, another meeting was held in the Bunbury rooms so the ratepayers and the Guardians could review the design by Saxon Snell. No one wanted this building that was being forced upon them by the Government. The angry ratepayers voiced their opinions, "*the proposed workhouse was too large, too expensive at a time when the district was suffering financially, in the wrong location and just unnecessary when the current workhouse could be brought up to required standards at a fraction of the cost".* Mr. Odden Frederic Read, a member of the Board of Guardians, agreed with all the points raised but reminded the room that on several occasions they have, *"requested to amend the current building and it has always been met with 'No'".*

Mildenhall was being forced into building a new workhouse to a design that would appease the Local Government Board, and if the ratepayers were going to foot the bill for a new building they were not prepared to have it in its current location. It was suggested that a new location be found, and that St. Andrews Street meadow be sold to fund the purchase of land elsewhere.

Mildenhall managed to hold off the enforced building project for several more years and it wasn't until 1893 that a new site was found and purchased. Following the sale of the St Andrews Street site, the Board of Guardians advertised in the local press for offers of land they could purchase for the new workhouse. The requirements were that it must be five to ten acres in size and be within a radius of three quarters of a mile from the market cross in Mildenhall Town Centre.

Mr. Bailey, a local landowner, offered seven acres of land in Cemetery Way (Kingsway) to the Board of Guardians for £460. The land was half a mile from the town centre, and at this time Kingsway was a dusty dirt road with fields and a row of trees neatly spaced out on both sides, forming a picturesque entry into this rural town. This location, on what was the outskirts of Mildenhall, was much more acceptable to the wealthy ratepayers than that of the St Andrew's Street site.

The Board of Guardians, having secured their new site, decided not to go ahead with the design by Henry Saxon Snell, which was originally designed for the St Andrew's site. Instead, they used the services of Frank Whitmore, who was an architect famous for his public buildings throughout the city of Chelmsford. Whitmore's buildings were known for fine brick and stone detailing.

In June 1894, the Board of Guardians placed an advertisement in the East Anglian Daily Times to announce that they were now prepared to receive tenders to build the new workhouse. The successful firm chosen for the contract was Kerridge and Shaw, a company from Cambridge who had been responsible for building many of the Victorian buildings in that city, including fire stations, schools and hotels. Kerridge and Shaw was owned and run by Charles Kerridge, an interesting character in his own right. Kerridge's wife passed away in 1880, aged just thirty-one years old, and on her deathbed she told him he should marry her sister, which he was more than happy to do. Just a few weeks after his wife had died, his five year old son also died after an accident on one of his building sites. You can only imagine the heartache Charles Kerridge felt in those few dreadful weeks.

By March 1895, building on the new workhouse had commenced. Mr. Vale, the landlord of the Maids Head, took full advantage and made an application to open earlier in the mornings so that he could benefit from the trade he would receive from the workmen of the building site. Mr Vale, in his application, said, *"100 to 120 men would be working on the site, the majority of whom would pass by my house. I could sell them coffee and cocoa as well as beer"*. The magistrates allowed the extended license and granted Mr. Vale permission to open between 5:00am and 6:00am on weekdays. Now, that sounds like an accident waiting to happen!

A report in the local paper from May 1895 gave an update on the building project, *"being built under compulsory order by the local government board. The building was now well under way, the original plans had been tweaked to enlarge the dining area, the roofing on the first block had already been commenced, the vagrant block on the opposite side of the entrance was just about ready for roofing and the main block had been started, the infirmary would be left till last."*

In November 1895, the Board of Guardians accepted a tender from Smith, Stiles and Mutton for the supply of workhouse furniture. The tradesman Mutton would have been E. J. Mutton, a local blacksmith, who worked from St Andrews-street in Mildenhall and would go on to purchase the old workhouse in the churchyard.

On 13th December 1895 the new workhouse had finally been completed at an astronomical cost of £11,000 which would be the equivalent of £1.5 million today. To mark the occasion, the Board of Guardians, along with representatives from the builders Kerridge and Shaw and the architect Frank Whitmore, held a celebration luncheon in the dining hall hosted by Odden Fredric Read, the Chairman of the Guardians. There was much back patting and congratulating each other before a toast of "The Queen" was given, as well as a toast to the Chairman and Vice Chairman of the Board of Guardians.

The workhouse was a very grand Victorian public building and the stone detailing for which Frank Whitmore was known was clearly present, and every bit as impressive as the Guardians could have hoped. It's a tragedy that this building is no longer present in the town today.

A detailed description was given in the Bury and Norwich post on Tuesday 17th December 1895:

"...approached from the main road through massive iron gates. On the right hand is the boardroom block, containing spacious board and committee rooms, clerks' room, waiting room and lavatory; on the left hand and opposite this building is the porter's lodge and tramp block for females and males, with day and night cells, association wards, receiving wards etc. Behind these is situated the main block, with the master's house in the centre, three stories high. The right wing two stories high, accommodates the female paupers and the left wing the male paupers, with necessary day rooms, dormitories, attendants' rooms etc. A range of buildings, one story high, flanking the male paupers contains the boys' day rooms, dormitories etc. And accommodation for married couples, with garden for each. At the back of the Master's house is the administrative block, containing spacious kitchen, scullery and stores for meat, bread, linen, clothes and dry goods; also a lofty dining hall and behind the kitchen is located the boiler house, coal house, and pump room. The boiler house contains two boilers for supplying the whole of the buildings with hot water and steam for the purposes of cooking, warming rooms and corridors and water supply to baths, sinks and laundry. The cold water supply is obtained from a well and forced by steam pumps to large tanks in the tank room, over the Master's house, and from thence it is distributed to various parts of the building. At the back of the grounds, completely isolated from all other buildings, are located the infirmary buildings, containing nurses' administrative department, with lying-in wards at the back, and right and left wings for male and female patients, with foul wards for each sex at the extreme ends quite distinct from general wards. A mortuary is erected on the west side of the site. Airing yards are provided for each sex in the different departments, bounded by high brick walls. All the baths, closets, slop sinks and other conveniences are up to date in design and all sanitary blocks are intercepted from main buildings by fresh air lobbies. All the different departments in the different blocks are connected by covered walk ways, so communication can be made between each without being exposed to wet weather. The rainwater is stored in a

large rainwater tank near the laundry block and all the sewage is conveyed to a tank at the extreme end of the site, and all necessary manholes, flushing tanks and interceptors provided on the most approved modern system. The buildings are built with Suffolk white bricks, and dressings quoins, molded courses and other finishings in red brick. The roofs are covered with slates."

CHAPTER FIVE

Meet the Jessups

The Jessups became a Mildenhall family and I'm sure there must be a few descendants of this family in the area today. Those most likely to be descendants of Edith Jessup are to be found in the Brandon area. However, over the years all eight surviving children of Charles and Sarah moved away from Mildenhall, and in just one generation Mildenhall lost the Jessup family name which had been so well known for so many years.

The Jessup family moved into the new Union Workhouse when it was completed in 1896. Space would no longer be an issue for the family. The new building, known locally as the "red house", was a giant Victorian mansion that would now be their home for the next 20 years. The Jessups bought land opposite the new workhouse where they had an orchard and later the two young Jessup brothers would have a garden and nursery business there.

It must have been a strange childhood growing up in a workhouse, but one that ensured the family were well cared for and financially secure. Charles became a wealthy man and acquired several pieces of land and property in the town and surrounding villages.

As the Jessup children grew up, they all started to work and live in the local area. The first to move out of the workhouse was the eldest child, Augustus, who in 1901 lived a stone's throw away in what was one of the newly built houses in Kingsway, making his living as a gardener. All the Jessup men evidently had green fingers!

Augustus found love. He had fallen in love with his first cousin, Frances Maud Bullard, the daughter of his mother's sister, Fanny Bullard. In 1904, the two of them emigrated to South Africa and married in Pietermaritzburg in the province of Natal. They settled in the area and had two children, Augustus George, born 1905, and Ivy Gladys, born 1907.

In August 1916, the young children lost their mother when Frances, who suffered from endometriosis, died after a short illness. The death of a young family's mother is always heartbreaking, no matter what the timing involved, but this was particularly bad timing. The First World War had just broken out. The British were at war and the South African army would fight alongside them. Augustus fought with the South African 4th Regiment, leaving from Cape Town aboard HMT Euripides in April 1917. Augustus had to leave his two young children, who were still grieving the death of their mother, while he went to fight in one of the bloodiest wars ever fought on this planet.

Wearing their uniquely green kilted uniform, with collar badges proudly bearing the motto "Mors Lucrum Mihi"—"Death is my reward", the South African 4th Regiment arrived in France on 15th July 1917. On arrival they proudly performed their African Tribal War Dance, joyfully dancing around and screaming with their bayonets drawn. Augustus, along with his regiment, was in action in September at Menin Road and at St Julien in October. Augustus was wounded in November that year at the Cambrai offensive, leaving him hospitalised until February 1918. After his release from hospital, Augustus returned to France to fight again, this time in the deadliest battle of the war, the battle of Somme, where Augustus was tragically killed in action in March 1918, leaving his young children orphaned.

The young South African Jessup children, aged eleven and thirteen, had lived through a horrendous year and a half, losing both parents to illness and war. Augustus left a Will which stated that, in the event of his death, his children should be handed over to his wife's sister, Beatrice Rolls (nee Bullard), who was living at 14 Normandy Road, London. A year later, in 1919, both children were listed as passengers on a ship arriving in Southampton for "permanent settlement". I wonder if Charles Jessup ever met his grandchildren once they arrived and settled in the UK.

Augustus Jessup is commemorated on the Mildenhall War Memorial as A. Jessup, although his name was not on the original monument at its unveiling in October 1920. It was added in January 1921, alongside an additional six names. Presumably Augustus was omitted as he had left Mildenhall and England, possibly being added later at the request of his family.

Charlotte (Lottie) Jessup was the eldest daughter, and in early adulthood she took on the role of Assistant Matron of the workhouse, a position she held in the 1901 census record. Later, Lottie left Mildenhall to become a nurse, working at the Middlesex Hospital in Marylebone, London.

After Charlotte left Mildenhall, her younger sister, Isabel, took over as Assistant Matron and is listed in this role in the 1911 census. It was not a role she fulfilled for very long, as in 1912 Miss Roper was appointed the Assistant Matron. In 1915, Isabel Jessup and her husband Charles Howson were appointed Porter and Portress of the workhouse at Elham, Kent. It is remarkable just how many of Charles Jessup's family members gave service to public institutions across the country.

In 1901, the 17-year-old Maude Edith Jessup was living with her parents at the workhouse while employed outside of the institution as a stationer's assistant. In 1906, Maude married her employer, Thomas Green, a stationer from Brandon. The 1951 newspaper obituary for Maude stated that she had been a stationer and newsagent in Brandon for the past 46 years and had also been one of the first female members of the Brandon parish council, being elected in 1946.

Florence Henrietta was the youngest daughter and, like her sister Maude, she married into a local family when she married Aubrey Rolph, the son of a Lakenheath farmer, in 1909. They later moved to Fengate, Weeting, before moving on to St Faith's and Aylsham district, North of Norwich where they farmed Grange Farm together.

The two youngest Jessup children, Alfred and Reginald Jessup, ran a nursery opposite the workhouse called "Red House Nurseries", where they grew fruit and vegetables. They also ran a florist business and supplied floral displays for local weddings.

In November 1914, the Jessup brothers found themselves in trouble for working a mare in an unfit state. On a freezing cold

November morning, Alfred loaded his cart with five hundredweight of fruit and vegetables. He readied his old mare, covering her seven bleeding sores under the saddle. This horse was not fit to walk the ten miles to Brandon, let alone pull a full cart. Alfred had made this same journey to Brandon every week during the war, selling his produce door to door, but he had a few weeks previously been warned not to work this old mare. The Jessup brothers' persistent working of the mare would see them end up in court. During their trial, they stated that they had to use this old mare due to the lack of horses in Mildenhall for hire at that time. The defendants were fined £1 and costs.

Alfred married Maud Roper in 1915, she being the daughter of the Assistant Matron of the workhouse. They moved away from the Mildenhall area and are listed on the 1939 register as residing in Slough with their child, Richard Jessup. Alfred's occupation is given as greengrocer, a career he had started in Mildenhall.

Reginald Jessup also left Mildenhall, moving to Nottinghamshire, where he became a police officer stationed at Kirkby in Ashfield. Like his father, he moved to a new town as a stranger before becoming fully immersed and accepted in the local life, his obituary noting that he was well respected and looked after the grounds of the War Memorial for many years. All the male Jessups had green fingers and were involved in gardening or fruit and vegetables at some time in their lives. I'm sure the grounds of Kirkby in Ashfield War Memorial looked stunning. He served as a policeman for twenty years before his death in 1949.

CHAPTER SIX

Odden Frederic Read 1849 – 1934

It seems strange, in a book about the poor of Mildenhall, to introduce a man who was born into a very wealthy family and lived in luxury throughout his life in one of the largest houses in the town. However, he is linked to every club or event that happened during his lifetime in Mildenhall—a true celebrity of the town's past.

The Read family were well known in Mildenhall, a respected family who shared their wealth and gave their time voluntarily for good causes. Odden Read's father, James Read, was a successful lawyer who volunteered as the church warden, a voluntary position he carried out for fifty-three years. Prior to the 1834 Poor Law Act, James Read was responsible for distributing the poor relief on behalf of Mildenhall Church. In 1834, he wrote to the Poor Law Commissioners, as the Mildenhall Poor Union had not yet been set up and he did not want to distribute a large sum of money without their direction. The Read family still leave their mark on St Mary's Church today. The pulpit, erected in 1875, was erected in memory of James Read, and the dedication alone shows how important the Read family were to the local community.

St Mary's Church has eight bells, all bearing wonderful inscriptions which detail when they were made, by whom and how they were funded. One of these bells is inscribed with James Read's name, immortalising his donation towards the bell.

John Taylor and Co., Loughborough,

James Read and Charles Owen

As Mildenhall residents, every time we hear these historic bells ring (the earliest dating to 1676), we know we can in part be thankful to the Read family for their donation. However, in 1897, at 3 o'clock one Sunday morning, the locals were not so thankful, as due to the clock running down, one of the church bells was continuously chiming, waking the town from its sleep.

In Mildenhall Churchyard, there stands the remains of an ancient building, which was once used as the charnel house. This ancient ruin predates many parts of the church. All that remains of this old building now is the entrance porch. The charnel house was used by the Read family as a family vault for over a century, the entrance porch being fitted with a large stone inscribed with the names of the members of the Read family who rest in the vault. Odden Read's brothers and sisters lay here, along with his father, James. The last member of his family inscribed on the stone is his sister, Jessie, who died in 1943. A family being allowed to use an ancient monument as a private vault would have to have been very wealthy and respected members of Mildenhall Town.

Odden Frederic Read was a successful family lawyer who, after qualifying in 1870, had carried on the practice of his father, who in turn had taken it over from his father, George Read, (Odden's grandfather). Like his father before him, Odden gave up his time to help the local community and donated money to many good causes.

It will be no surprise to learn that Odden became "Chairman of the Board of Guardians" for the Mildenhall Union, the Board of Guardians being responsible for administration of the Poor Law. They were elected by landowners who were liable for paying the poor rate —the tax which was used to provide poor relief. The Guardians were elected each year, although the term was increased to three years in 1894. Odden was a member of the Board of Guardians for over fifty years, which in itself demonstrates how popular he was amongst those voting for the board members.

Odden Read was possibly one of the most influential and important figures in the history of Mildenhall, and anyone carrying out research on any subject related to the town is very likely to come across his name very early on.

He was a member of so many local clubs and was voted onto so many local boards that he would work all day, followed by meetings every evening for various organisations in which he was involved. It is almost impossible to list all the public appointments that he held, but the list shown below, although nowhere near complete, demonstrates what an important and well-liked man he was in Mildenhall.

Public Appointments:

- Chairman of the Board of Guardians for over fifty years.
- Church Warden for over fifty years. (as was his father, James Read)
- Chairman of Directors of Mildenhall Town Hall.
- Chairman Mildenhall Voluntary School managers.
- Chairman Mildenhall and District Horticultural Society.
- Clerk to local old age pensions committee.
- Director Mildenhall Gas Company.
- Chairman Lark Angling Society.
- Mildenhall Rural District Councillor.
- Coroner for Thetford for more than sixty years.
- Member of the Masons since 1872.
- Member of Mildenhall Conservative Association.

When Odden Read passed away in 1934, at the age of eighty-six, there were over eighty floral tributes at his funeral. He had been involved with so much that had happened in Mildenhall during his lifetime, that his loss touched the whole of the town. On the evening of his funeral, the church bells were rung in his honour, the flag on the top of St Mary's Church was flown at half-mast throughout the day and the blinds of local Mildenhall businesses and those of private residents were drawn during the time of the funeral. The Voluntary Schools in Mildenhall, in which Odden was actively involved, were all closed for the afternoon.

The following passages, taken from the Bury Free Press of 10th March, 1934, were part of an in-depth report of the life and death of Odden Fredric Read:

"Mr. Read was in many respects a remarkable man. Upright, and with much more vigour than some men many years his junior"......"He would easily have passed for quite 10 years less than his age".....Mr. Read continued to do a full day's work and also took a prominent part — as had done for many years — in the

public and social life of that pretty little country town of Mildenhall. Mr. Reed was a typical English country gentleman, dignified and kindly, with a ready wit and a sunny disposition, and one had only to watch him round about his own town to see how popular he was with people of all classes. It is no exaggeration to say that he was the type of Englishman that anywhere and everywhere enhances the reputation of our country."

In 1895 when the new Union workhouse was built in Kingsway, Odden Read had the honor of laying the foundation stone, a stone that would commemorate his name in Mildenhall for years to come.

In 1930, there was a series of articles in the Bury Free Press interviewing "People in the public eye", and on the 3rd May, 1930, it focused on Odden Read. In this interview, Mr. Read mentions how lucky he had been to have laid the workhouse foundation stone, and now, years later, to have the same stone in his garden. A record of that interview shows:

"Mr. Read recalled that he had for nearly 50 years been a Guardian, and that he had the honour of laying the foundation stone of the Workhouse in Kingsway, Mildenhall. That same stone, he said, was now in his garden, where it was placed on demolition of the workhouse some years ago."

Reading this article ignited my imagination. Was it possible that this foundation stone was still somewhere in Mildenhall? It was a slim hope as I had never seen, heard or read about it. Could it still be in what was Odden Read's garden? Where did he live? Was the house even still there? At the time of discovering this article, I had not done any research on Odden Read, as I was still concentrating on the inmates. In fact, at that time I had very little interest in researching a rich, wealthy "non-inmate"—it didn't fit within the scope of my research.

I paused my research on the poor and immediately switched my attention to Odden Read and the whereabouts of the foundation stone. I searched for Odden Read in the census records of 1901 and 1911, and found that on both occasions, he was living at West Street with his second wife, two of his seven children (who were different on each census record) and two servants. I knew that West Street was now named Queensway. It didn't take much imagination to think that he must have lived in a large residence. In my mind, I was recalling all the larger homes that I could remember down this street.

Reading through the census records, I tried to follow the route in my mind, retracing the route that the census taker would have travelled one hundred and twenty years ago. As I travelled down West Street, I passed the Prince of Wales public house, the Manor house and Wamil Road walking up to the Gardeners' Arms before doubling back. I could now roughly position Odden Read's house on the street from the buildings listed around it. Odden Read's home was at the opposite end of the street to the public houses, The Queen's Arms and Gardeners' Arms, just past the Prince of Wales public house and next to or opposite the Manor house. I had narrowed down the location to just a few houses where it could have been.

So, I traveled back in time another decade to 1891, when this census record showed that the Read family were still living at West Street. However, the audit taker had this time written more detail next to the Odden residence. Written next to Odden Read's name was the name of his house, "The Limes". The Reads' neighbours were listed as the Manor house, occupied by Frances Joanna Bunbury, the widow of Sir Charles Bunbury who had died five years previously, along with several of her family members and a long list of staff. In total, twenty-two people were present at the Manor house during the 1891 census. It was a grand Tudor house that, sadly, was demolished in the 1930s.

Mr. Read, in 1891, was living with his wife and five children, a governess and three servants. I knew that if "The Limes" was a house that still existed today I couldn't miss it—a large building located very close to the former Manor house site.

In the Bury Free Press, I found a newspaper article dated 28th April, 1934, one month after Odden Read's death. It is a list of furniture located at "The Limes", which was being sold under instruction from the Executors of Odden Read. The items listed conjure up images of how grand this house must have looked inside as well as outside. Rooms populated with antique mahogany furniture, a rosewood grand piano, silver tableware and ornate clocks. The advertisement for the auction carried out by local auctioneer Mr. F G Parker, was listed as below:

"The Limes"
West Street
Mildenhall
Sale of Antique & other Furniture
Including: 8ft Mahogony Wardrobe, Birch Bedroom Suite, Handsome

Mahogony Dining Table, 3 Large Antique Chairs. Georgian Mahogany Pedestal Sideboard, 3 Antique Mahogony Side-Tables, 2 Antique Carved Oak Chests, 3 ft Sheraton Writing Table, enclosed by roll top, Oak Bible Box, 2 Jacobean Oak Court Cupboards, Boulle Clock, Broadwood Grand Pianoforte in Rosewood, Plate and Silver, and a number of XVIII Century and early XIX Century Volumes of local and antiquarian interest etc. which

MR. F. G. Parker

Is instructed by the Executors of the Late Odden F Read Esq. to Sell by Auction, in a marqueee (sic) upon the premises, on

THURSDAY, 10th May, 1934,

Commencing at Ten O'clock prompt.

On View Wednesday afternoon. May 9th.

Catalogues of the Auctioneer, Mildenhall .

Odden Fredric Read was also the owner of a diary which he had inherited from his father, James Read. The diary was that of a famous inhabitant of the Mildenhall parish, William Coe, known as Squire Coe to the locals, a wealthy man whose family had made their money from the Suffolk cloth trade. The diary covers William Coe's life from December 1693 to May 1729. In the diary, Coe details his late nights at the Cock Inn in Mildenhall—often with Sir Thomas Hanmer. There is a running theme in the diary that Coe regrets many of his actions from the night before and the next day asks forgiveness for his sins. It's a fascinating diary that gives an insight into Coe's life and the life of a rich gentleman of Mildenhall in Georgian England. It details the struggles he faced from being a deeply religious man who was far too easily tempted by everything on offer afforded to him by his immense wealth. This diary was donated to Cambridge University in 1935 by Odden Fredric Read's son and is still part of their manuscript collection today.

One of Squire Coe's many diary entries, which spawned a poem, is now sadly missing. In 1700, Coe had commissioned a wig to be made out of his eldest three daughters' hair. In 1869, extracts of Coe's diary were printed in a publication called "The Athenaeum" for an event that took place in Bury St Edmunds that year, and the entry about Coe's wig was included. A poem written by Mortimer Collins in 1871 was based on this entry. The diary entry detailing Coe's wig also appeared in A.E. Simpson's "History of Mildenhall" in 1892:

"1700, February 14th.

Mr. Eldred of Bury cut off my girls' hair, Judith, Anne and Elizabeth, to make a wig, 1 1/2 ounces bare weight"

However, in 1895, it was reported that this entry could no longer be found in the diary, and it was also not included in the transcribed version of the diary that was published in the East Anglian in 1906 - 1907. The page was no longer present in the original diary and had been cut out. Did Odden Fredric Read remove this page while the book was in his possession? Luckily the Squire Coe story lives on in the 1871 poem by Mortimer Collins:

Flat is the Shire of the Southern folk,
And its streams are sluggish, very,
And they say you never heard a joke
In the town of St. Edmund's Bury.
But that's a story too absurd
To satisfy Psychologists,
And I guess that numerous jokes were heard
In the days of Archaeologists
When light was shown on topics dark,
Beside the lazy river Llark.
A golden shire of plenteous corn,
Which in August-tide grows yellow,
And for jolly Squires that wheat is shorn
Who love old ale and mellow.
But from ancient habits well men know,
In these days we vastly vary,
And where's Squire Coe of fair West Row,
In the days of William and Mary;
The Squire who with punch defied all care,
And made a wig with his daughters' hair.
Lo, where they sit, those maidens three,
A sight for young beholders,
With viol or book upon shapely knee,
Long locks over rose-white shoulders;
No trace of grief in their mien appears,
And they look demurely merry,
Though they wait alas for the fatal shears
That the barber brings from Bury;
No fainter Anglians ere drew breath,

Than Judith, Anne, Elizabeth.
Ah! What would say the Suffolk girl,
In these days of advanced opinion,
If asked to yield but one curl
That veils her voluminous chignon?
What Suffolk Squire though never a hair
His sterile scalp can harbour,
To share his daughters' tresses dare
Send for the Bury barber?
'Tis well Squire Coe in the mould lies low,
For this is a world he scarce would know.

I hadn't thought about the workhouse foundation stone or "The Limes" again, until a few mornings later. I woke at 2 a.m. and was not able to get back to sleep, lying in bed thinking about my research when I suddenly had a recollection about the name "The Limes". I cannot explain why this memory suddenly came to me in the early hours of the morning, or why it had not surfaced previously, but suddenly I had a vague memory of seeing a sign on a gate that said "The Limes" in front of a large Georgian-looking house. The house which I was thinking of was now converted into flats, and I can see it from my bedroom window. I wondered if my memory of seeing this sign was correct or was my mind playing tricks on me at 2 a.m. after days of over thinking.

The next morning, on my way to work, I took a detour and passed this building. I pulled over in the rush hour traffic and parked on the side of the road. I walked up to the gate and straight away noticed what looked like the original Victorian house sign tied to the gate. The copper name plate itself still looked relatively tidy—a pressed sign with a hammered finish spelling out "THE LIMES", complete with a lovely green patina from over one hundred years out in the elements. The rest of the sign was looking quite sorry and neglected. The name plate had three of its original six screws remaining, just about attaching it to a rotting, grey and weathered piece of wood. To quote an old Suffolk saying, "it's sitting slightly on the huh". I like to think this sign has been hanging here slowly declining since the day Odden Read placed it there.

I started to look for what would have been Odden's front garden, in the hope that the stone could have been left sitting in a corner, forgotten by time, hidden by plants, shrubs or weeds, where it had sat for the last ninety years. I quickly found there was no longer a front garden as it had been dug up and turned into parking for the flats that now occupy the former Read residence. As I stood looking at the grand building, imagining Odden coming and going from the large front door, I noticed a large inscribed stone set in the wall surrounding the house, which read:

THIS STONE WAS LAID

BY

O. F. READ

CHAIRMAN OF THE BOARD

OF GUARDIANS

JULY 24TH 1895

I found it! This was definitely the workhouse foundation stone. Along with Odden Read's name, it also had the name of both the builders and architect responsible for the design and construction of the workhouse. In the 1930 Bury Free Press article, Odden Read had said the stone was in his garden, but did he say "garden" in a nonspecific way, when all the time he had laid it in his own wall? Or was the stone laid in his wall after his death in 1934? Looking back at old photos of West Street, this wall was surrounded by large lime trees (which are long since gone), so it seemed unlikely Odden would have placed the stone in this wall.

I was not sure if anyone locally was aware that the foundation stone of the Union Workhouse was still in existence, long outliving the building itself, located in an altogether different part of Mildenhall. It looked, for all intents and purposes, that the stone laid in its new position was referencing the house in front of which it sits, so why would anyone know of its connection to the old workhouse at the opposite end of Mildenhall?

After a quick Google search, I did discover the name of the current owner of this large Georgian building, which is still known as "The Limes". I sent an email to the owner, hoping that maybe he knew more about the foundation stone and how it had come to be in the wall. Was it there when he purchased the property? Or was it in the garden where Odden had talked of it in 1930?

I was soon to find out! The present owner did know more of this story and was willing to tell me all he knew about it. In the 1980s, the house next door to "The Limes" (14a Queensway) was built on what would have been part of "The Limes" garden, over the top of an old tennis court. The present owner changed the layout of the driveway and needed to demolish the existing driveway of number 14a.

When demolishing the driveway, the foundation stone was found built into the driveway, so, the current owner on taking it up was unsure what to do with this large stone. He quite rightfully thought it would be a criminal act to throw the stone in the rubble skip. He eventually decided it would be a good idea to lay the stone in the wall surrounding "The Limes".

I asked the owner if he was aware that the stone was from the workhouse, to which he replied that he had thought the stone was probably from the buildings opposite which had belonged to the Manor, demolished in the 1930s. I told the current owner how Odden Read had lived in his house and how the foundation stone had come to be at "The Limes" after Mr. Read had taken the foundation stone back to his house to place in his garden when the workhouse demolition started in 1924.

"The Limes" was sold shortly after Odden Read's death in 1934, and it has since been sold numerous times and had many alterations. "The Limes" once had extensive gardens that are all now built over, and in fact, my own house sits at what would have been the bottom of Odden Read's garden. It's amazing that after all this activity and loss of grounds, the foundation stone was not lost or discarded and has found its way back into a wall where it can hopefully sit for many years to come.

I still believe no one locally knows or is aware of the significance of this stone, or even that the workhouse foundation stone still exists. It was fortunate that the current owner of "The Limes" had the awareness and respect for the history of Mildenhall to have laid this stone into a wall. This wall is part of a conservation area and should therefore protect the stone for years to come.

The solicitor firm that had been set up by Odden Fredric Read's grandfather, George Read, continued after his death, changing the name to Carter and Jessop, and then in 1961, Gross & Co. purchased and operated it until the business was finally closed in 1999. Until 1999, the business had operated out of a purpose-built office that Odden Read had built, located at number four, Church Walk. When

Gross and Co. closed in 1999, a number of Wills were discovered in the loft—no one at the firm had ever seen them before or even knew that they existed. The first Will in the collection was dated 1769, and the last Will was dated at the end of 1933. It makes perfect sense that Odden Read had placed these Wills in the loft, and after his death in March 1934, no more were added or touched again until their discovery in 1999. These Wills are now kept by the Mildenhall Museum.

Mildenhall Town has a blue plaque heritage trail, where local points of interest and buildings are marked with a plaque detailing how it fits into the history of Mildenhall. Anyone can collect a trail leaflet from the Museum or bus station, follow the walk and discover these plaques. I'm sure if the creators of this brilliant walk had been aware that this foundation stone still existed, it also would be commemorated by a blue plaque for people to discover. I would also argue that Odden Fredric Read is well worthy of his own plaque, maybe above the door of "The Limes". It might not be an official plaque or part of the heritage trail, but as my own small commemoration to Odden Read, I have refurbished the original "THE LIMES" sign, mounted it on a replacement wooden base and hung it back on the gate as straight as the day Odden Read originally placed it there. No longer does it sit neglected, slightly on the huh!

CHAPTER SEVEN

William Sparke 1825 - 1903

William Sparke was an evil, vicious man who fully deserved his five years in the county goal. William was born into a hardworking family of blacksmiths where he also worked as a blacksmith. It was a physically demanding occupation that shaped William's strong, muscular physique, which he used as a weapon to intimidate and bully others. William later fell into poverty through poor decision making and poor drinking habits, which resulted in his long-term residence in the workhouse. It does not sit comfortably with me to say that any individual deserved the poor quality of life served up by the workhouse, but if anyone deserved a day of oakum picking followed by a supper of gruel, it was William Sparke.

William Sparke was a workhouse inmate at both the old building in the church yard where he appeared on the 1891 census, as well as the new Victorian-built Union Workhouse on Kingsway, where he was transferred following its completion in 1895 and was still present at the time of the 1901 census.

William's life began in 1825, in the village of Barton Mills, when he was born to parents John and Rachel Sparke. His mother, Rachel, originated from Cheveley near Newmarket. William's ancestors on his father's side (Sparke) had been present in the Barton Mills area since the early 18th century, when Barton Mills was still known by its original name of Barton Parva. The Sparke family had migrated to Mildenhall from Great Waldingfield in Suffolk, where they had been present since records became available.

In the 1891 census, ninety-seven Sparke families were living in Suffolk, more than any other English county. If you travelled back in time to this year and gathered all the people named Sparke (which would be a terrible use of a time machine), 31% of them would have been found in East Anglia, and more than 50% of those East Anglian Sparkes were living in Suffolk, a proper Suffolk family. *"Now thas a rum owd dew."*

William, or Bill as his family called him, was the first child of John and Rachel Sparke, but they did go on to have a further five children together, before John's premature death at the age of forty-seven.

William's youngest sister, Sarah Ann, had disabilities from birth, and was listed as deaf and dumb on the 1851 census. She was later labeled as an imbecile on the 1871 census, which took place just a few months before Sarah Ann passed away.

William's eldest sister, Elizabeth, had spent fourteen days at the St Marylebone Workhouse in 1853, where she gave birth to her second child. It was common practice for workhouses to be used as local hospitals, and many women used the workhouse for its lying-in ward (now called a labour ward). The pregnant ladies using these workhouses had usually been either too poor to have their baby at home or had no family support due the illegitimate nature of their pregnancy. In the case of Elizabeth Sparke, she was an unmarried woman giving birth to not just an illegitimate child, but her second illegitimate child.

Childbirth in Victorian England was a frighteningly perilous experience. There was no pain relief other than opium, which was very rarely used and a risk of mortality from complications during or after the birth. Women would even prepare for their own death prior to giving birth, and children would be sent to relatives so they did not have to hear the screams of childbirth endured without pain relief.

Unmarried mothers and their infants, in the eyes of the Victorians, were seen as a crime against morality. They were spurned and shunned by society. Once born, the child itself was stigmatised, considered to have inherited the parents' lack of moral character. The parents of other children would fear this illegitimate child might infect the morals of their own legitimate children. Family and friends of the woman would soon disappear if she fell pregnant outside of marriage and could not be relied upon to offer any form of support or help. If a young woman became pregnant while still living at home, she was often forced to leave the family in disgrace and move to an area where she was not known.

The Sparkes were a family of blacksmiths who lived and worked at "the Street", Barton Mills, in a house that still stands today. Not only had William's father been a blacksmith but so too had his mother. The vast majority of females at this time were listed in housekeeping roles, either paid or unpaid. Rachel Sparke was a bit of an anomaly in being a blacksmith, rare but not unique. In 1851, there were twelve thousand blacksmiths in England, and one hundred and fifty of those blacksmiths were female.

William and his brother James both followed their parents in becoming blacksmiths. In 1848, when their father, John Sparke, died, Rachel remarried. Her new husband, Joseph Holmes, as you may have guessed, was also a blacksmith. There would have been no shortage of horseshoes at their wedding, although unbeknown to Rachel at this time, they wouldn't be bringing her any luck!

The union of Sparke blacksmiths extended beyond William's immediate family; his uncle, Richard Sparke, who was living just a few doors down the street, was also a blacksmith, along with William's cousins Arthur, Richard and Sailsbury. Sailsbury was not a conventional man and didn't see himself as a blacksmith, as on census records he listed himself as a costermonger.

Costermongers were unlicensed mobile traders often selling their goods out of a wheelbarrow, basket or cart. Their target customers were the poorer members of society, and costers sold their goods at locations convenient to the lower classes. Costermongers attracted customers through their melodic sales patter, poems and chants. The sound of the costermonger could be heard throughout towns in England, and they were an iconic part of Victorian streets. There were many attempts by the authorities to remove costermongers, but public support was always very strongly in favour of the costermonger. The public appreciated the service and entertainment they offered, which helped the coster community survive attempts to eradicate them from the streets.

Being a costermonger was more than an occupation; it was a society, and most costermongers were from a performance background or fancied themselves as poets. In the case of Sailsbury Sparke, he was the self-proclaimed poet of Barton Mills. Costermongers wore clothing that was loud, bold and distinctive to draw attention to themselves. The coster dress code was a large neckerchief known as a Kingsman, a long waist coat and bell bottom trousers, their footwear decorated with thistle or heart motifs. The most famous fashion accessories of the costermonger were the mother of pearl buttons, which they would use to decorate their trousers. This coster tradition became more and more exaggerated until jackets and trousers were covered in shiny patterns created by mother of pearl buttons. People who wore these elaborately decorated jackets and trousers were known as pearly Kings or Queens, one of the most iconic and famous fashions to have ever come out of London—a fashion that belonged to the working class.

Sailsbury Sparke was in no way a successful poet, so his work is not easy to find. In fact, it simply did not survive. However, generations later, a poem was donated to Mildenhall Museum, found amongst some old family papers by a Mr. Bell, and it seems to be the only surviving piece of Sailsbury's poetry. Titled "Lines on Martha Fletcher", it is a poem that tells the true-life story of Sailsbury's friend who found herself as an unclaimed corpse in Mildenhall Workhouse. Sadly, in Victorian times, unclaimed bodies could be sold by the workhouse to universities for dissection and training of medical students.

The poor feared dying in the workhouse—robbed of their dignity whilst alive, they now had to fear the indignity of being dissected if they were unfortunate enough to die in the workhouse. The demand for the bodies required by medical science was far greater than the supply of bodies. This resulted in a profitable trade of dead bodies, and groups of men, who became known as resurrectionists, were snatching the bodies of the freshly buried and making a very healthy profit. The trade in dead bodies was so lucrative that men were willing to murder others so that they could sell their victims to universities and hospitals. The most famous case was that of Burke and Hare, who murdered and sold sixteen victims.

In 1832, to stop the illegal trade of cadavers, the Anatomy Act was introduced. This act permitted anyone in lawful possession of a dead body to allow it to be dissected. The "legal possession" clause of this

Act could be applied to hospitals, prisons and workhouses. It enabled a lucrative revenue for the workhouses, and they became an important provider of dead bodies for medical students.

For many years, Martha Fletcher had been a barmaid at the Anchor Inn in Tuddenham. This public house, which used to stand on the edge of the village green, has long since been demolished and replaced with modern houses. Martha had been employed by Philip Rumbelow, who was the landlord of the Anchor Inn. For many years, Martha had lived with the landlord's widowed mother, Mary Rumbelow, in a separate house beside the pub. In 1885, times got hard for Martha when Mary Rumbelow passed away and Philip Rumbelow left the Anchor Inn and moved to Bury St Edmunds. Martha Fletcher, now sixty-five years old, was left homeless and could not survive off her own means. There was no pension system at this time, and the only way for Martha to claim any form of relief was to admit herself to the Mildenhall Union Workhouse. Martha would have known that there would be no way out of the workhouse and that she would eventually die there. With no family to claim her body, she would have also known that once she left this world, there was every chance that she would end up being dissected for medical training or experimentation. In 1888, Martha died in the old Mildenhall Workhouse in the churchyard. Her body was unclaimed, and as the workhouse was in "legal possession" of her body, they sold it to Cambridge University. Sailsbury Sparke, learning of his friend's demise, wrote the following poem:

Lines On Martha Fletcher

Martha Fletcher was a village maid, industrious neat and clean,
At the Anchor Inn poor Martha stayed, which stands near Tuddenham Green.
Her master and her mistress, it grieved poor Martha sore,
At last with many a bitter sigh, passed in the workhouse door.
On uncooked meat, the coarsest fare, she existed for a while,
Without a friend's domestic tear, she died in durance vile.
They call this land civilised, Oh! That's a horrid word.
Poor Martha was anatomised, worse than a heaven served.
Our soldiers on the battle field, all dangers they will brave
Their fallen comrades they will shield, in a cold and silent grave.
The parsons in the pulpit stand, there they preach and pray,
Pointing out the heavenly land and showing all the way.

But when the Poor Law Board they go on, they appear with faces bold.
Sell our daughters and our sons for the gain of paltry gold.
In dissecting rooms with limbs all bare, before cannibals young and gay,
Like cannibals they cut and tear, and glory in the bloody fray.
'Tis thus our daughters dear are treated, by men of this cruel world,
Of a cold and silent grave defeated, who will sell our bodies and souls.
This Eastertide they'll all be preaching about our doom in long years hence,
Recollect, oh man, that all teaching is for shillings, pounds and pence.
We pray, of God - look on this wrong with pitying eye, and quickly too
Sympathise with an oppressed throng that's filled with grief and bitter woe.
Inspire hard hearts to deeds sublime, teach them like Christians to behave.
Be with our souls at eventide, grant us a cold and silent grave.

S.P Sparke, Barton Mills
April 14th 1888.

Sailsbury Sparke had also been an inmate of the workhouse. Perhaps selling fruit and vegetables to the poor was not the money spinner of which he had dreamed, or maybe his poetry was not as popular as he had hoped. On leaving the workhouse, Sailsbury and another former workhouse inmate, described only as a blind butcher (now that doesn't sound safe), decided to travel to London to protest to the Poor Law Commissioners about the treatment of inmates at the Mildenhall Workhouse. Sailsbury, who had a lame leg, sat in his wheelbarrow and was pushed by his blind friend. This was reported in the Bury Free Press in 29th September, 1888:

"The Blind and the Lame

Last Monday morning two recent inmates of the Mildenhall Union house —
Sailsbury Sparke, the crippled blacksmith who generally styles himself the
"Barton Mills' poet", and a blind butcher —started from Barton Mills, the blind
man wheeling the lame one in a barrow, their object being to get to London and
lay before the Government some complaints about workhouse management. They
arrived at Newmarket on Monday night, and Cambridge on Tuesday, leaving
Cambridge for Royston on Thursday."

In the 1850s, William Sparke, aged 25 years, left the family home and moved further afield to Birmingham, taking advantage of the thriving metal work industry that was booming in the city. William lived away from Suffolk for some years, earning a decent wage for his metalworking skills, which were in high demand as cities and industry expanded.

William Sparke had been away earning city money for about twenty years before he moved back to Suffolk. In 1871, William's mothers' second husband and William's young disabled sister had both died, and his mother, Rachel, was now living alone in a house on "the street in Barton Mills. William moved in with Rachel, providing him with a place to live while also being able to provide for himself and his elderly mother by working locally—once again as a blacksmith.

This living arrangement existed harmoniously for a few years, a seemingly convenient and mutually beneficial arrangement, but William's bad temper was a ticking time bomb that would destroy this harmony. On Good Friday of 1885, William's anger erupted in an explosive fit of violence that would shatter both their lives.

On the Friday morning of April 3rd, 1885, Rachel had lovingly cooked her son breakfast before they left for Good Friday church service. William's mother had already laid the table with breakfast and was sitting in a chair waiting for her son to join her. As William entered the room, Rachel looked up at her son and said "Bill, you have not washed your hands". What seemed like an innocent request sent William into an uncontrollable rage—it was the spark that set off Sparke!

William, according to his mother's testimony in court, looked at her with an offensive expression before walking over to the hearth and picking up the iron poker, before turning and striking her over the head with it four times.

Rachel was now sitting in a pool of blood close to death. Having released all his anger through the iron poker, William was now calmer and resumed seeing sense. William knew he had to get to the police station and explain what he had done, so before leaving he knocked on the door of his neighbour, Mr. Pledger, who also happened to be a blacksmith.

In court, Mr. Pledger recalled the prisoner coming to his house about 8.35 a.m., shouting, "Charlie, I want you. Me and the old woman have had a row, I want you to go see her". Mr. Pledger said it was nothing to do with him and he would not go, but William continued to ask him and followed him into his yard, begging him to go look at his mother.

Mr. Pledger again said, "No".

William responded, "Stop till I pick my stick up. I am off to Mildenhall". He went on to say, "She aggravated me so I struck her across the head with a poker".

Mr. Pledger gave in and went next door, where he gave the following account: "I found her sitting on the chair bleeding from the head, she was partly conscious, the blood was flowing to her lap and from thence to the floor". I said, "Whatever is the matter?" Her eyes were open and breakfast was on the table. She replied "Oh, he struck me with the poker two or three times". I saw a poker laying on the hearth which was bent, two weeks previously I had to re-lay the poker, I never see a poker so peculiarly bent as this one."

The red mist of rage had cleared and with Mr. Pledger sitting with his mother, William set off on his journey to Mildenhall Police Station, which at that time was still situated in Police Station Square. The building has since been a courthouse and is now a vets.

William arrived at the Police Station at 9.30 a.m. and spoke to the superintendent on duty, Samuel Garnham Reeve.

At the trial, Samuel Garnham Reeve gave the following account: "The Prisoner came to the police station about 9.30, and he said, "I have come to give myself up". I asked his name and address, which he gave. I said "What have you done?"

He said "Me and my mother had a quarrel, I struck her across the head with a poker".

I said, "Good Gracious, you have not been killing the woman?"

He said, "I don't know, I am sure".

I told the prisoner I would charge him with brutally assaulting his mother with a poker.

He said, "She took up the poker first, I snatched it away from her and struck her on the head".

Dr Pelham Aldrich, the local doctor who lived in Clinton House in Mill Street, was called to attend to Rachel at her house. The following account is that of Dr Pelham Aldrich:

"About half past nine o'clock this morning, I was asked to attend Rachel Holmes at Barton Mills, and I found her suffering from four separate wounds on the head, lacerated and contused wounds. Three of them were down to the bone of the skull. I have now examined her and believe she is not likely, in my opinion, to recover".

Mr. A. W. T. Angrove, another surgeon at Mildenhall, also attended Mrs. Holmes that morning:

"I went to Mrs. Holmes' house and found her in the kitchen sitting on a chair in a semi-conscious condition... She showed signs of congestion, she was sick and seemed as if she would have died".

His lordship: "She may be dead now for anything you know?"

Witness: "She may be, but I find that unlikely".

His Lordship asked Dr. Angrove if the injured woman was in a condition to talk about what happened.

Dr. Angrove said, "Yes".

"Does she blame herself for it?"

"Not at all".

"For having provoked the violence?"

"Not at all, she distinctly contradicts the statement his snatching the poker from her".

Dr. Angrove said he understood that Sparke had been away from Mildenhall for some years, earning high wages, but he returned four years ago without any money and had been living on his mother. He had been very morose in his manners and unkind in his ways. He had slight paralysis of the brain and was believed to have drunk a great deal.

The jury in William Sparke's court case found him guilty of wounding with intent to cause grievously bodily harm, but not guilty of the charge of wounding with intent to murder. William saw out the rest of his life in a miserable existence, starting with five years in the County Gaol in Ipswich, followed by thirteen years in the Mildenhall Union Workhouse.

William Sparke is a man who appears to be from a good hard-working family, a man who was fortunate to earn "high wages", according to evidence from his 1885 trial. It seems that he had returned to Mildenhall after his time away, penniless, a drunk and with paralysis of the brain.

Paralysis of the brain in the Victorian era was a diagnosis that was given to thousands of people across the country, the majority in their thirties or forties. The prognosis was poor, and many of these people would die within months of a diagnosis. The disease would cause the person to become violent and slur their speech, alter their walk to a stagger and cause muscular weakness. Asylums across England had patients with these symptoms, men who were seemingly fine, suddenly cut down in their prime and sent to Asylums leaving their family behind.

Studies found that those affected with paralysis of the brain were mainly men, with military men particularly susceptible, yet men of the clergy were not affected. Women infected were often found to be prostitutes or those innocently infected by cheating husbands. A link was found between ports, mining towns and industrialised towns. Eventually, it was acknowledged that paralysis of the brain and syphilis were almost certainly linked. In 1905, a test for syphilis was developed, and men in asylums with the diagnosis of paralysis of the brain were tested with many positive test results. It had been found that untreated syphilis would eventually attack the brain, leaving its victims helpless.

Could William have caught syphilis from his time working away in industrial towns? The evidence suggests this could have been likely. Cases of paralysis of the brain and syphilis decreased in the 1940s, when penicillin was discovered and widely used, often curing the disease before people even knew they had it. Ironically, penicillin was discovered by a man well known in Barton Mills, the Scottish physician Sir Alexander Fleming, who from 1921 until his death in 1955, owned a house in Barton Mills opposite that where William Sparke had lived. Alexander Fleming's house, named "Dhoon", is still present in the village today.

William Sparke's entry into the nominal register for Ipswich Gaol does not tell us a great deal more than we already know about the man. When looking up this entry, I was really hoping there would be a photo or sketch of either William or his distinguishing features. I have even seen some prison records that exist where they have taken the time to sketch the tattoos of prisoners. Other than the details of his crime, William's record only tells us he was 5'7 ¼, (which was a couple of inches taller than the average height for a male of the time) and he had grey hair, which is no surprise as he was sixty years old at the time of the attack.

Rachel, against the odds, recovered from the attack and lived another six years, dying on 10th April, 1891. The 1891 census, which was taken five days before her death, shows her living at 21 The

Rectory, Barton Mills. On the day of the census, her daughters Eliza (now Eliza Ison) and Elizabeth (now Elizabeth Pridgeon) were visiting her. Living away from Suffolk, they had travelled back at the same time to be with their mother. With Rachel dying five days later, I think it is a fair assumption they were visiting their mother to say goodbye to her and nurse her during her final hours.

Many of the workhouse inmates were there due to desperation caused by circumstances over which they had no control. Orphans, widows, the lame, the blind and those suffering mental illness are just a few examples of people in situations caused by bad luck rather than bad choices, which all led to workhouse admittance. The desperate and destitute of Mildenhall had no choice but to accept the tough conditions of the workhouse, carrying out tedious or back breaking work in return for some very basic food and a shared bedroom, often even a shared bed.

William did have a choice; he had a job, he had a home and could have lived comfortably, free from the confinement of both the prison and workhouse. It was William's unhinged violent nature and an anger that he unleashed on his mother that caused his plight, a totally self-inflicted path down which he chose to walk. His horrendous crime cost him five years in the county goal, and following his release, he was sucked into a poverty vacuum dragging him into the workhouse, a poverty trap that a man of his age would never be able to escape. William died at the workhouse in 1903 at the age of seventy-eight, but before his death he found himself yet again on trial following a fit of rage which this time resulted in the death of an inmate. We will meet this poor soul in our next chapter.

CHAPTER EIGHT

John Trudgett 1835 – 1896

They say you only live once, so make the most of it! John Trudgett's one life came and went, and despite his best efforts to make the most of it, his life was full of gloom, death, tragedy and sadness. John had already dealt his fair share of bad luck well before he was unfortunate enough to be placed in a room with fellow workhouse inmate, William Sparke.

John Trudgett was a miller from the village of Lakenheath, born to James and Ann Trudgett (nee Gathercole) in 1835. They were a farming family from Lakenheath. The Trudgetts owned a windmill in the village, one of three windmills that were in Lakenheath at the time. John's father, James Trudgett, worked the mill in Undley-road, Lakenheath, in an area known as The Claypits. As well as working the mill, the Trudgett family (comprising John, his parents, sisters Elizabeth and Mary and his younger brother, James) all lived at the mill. The 1851 census shows that at 16 years of age, John is listed as a miller along with his father.

In 1853, John Trudgett would have had the unique opportunity to attend a heavyweight bare knuckle boxing match in the village of Lakenheath. For some bizarre reason, Lakenheath, a tiny village with a handful of farmers (and millers evidently), was chosen as the venue for the Sayers and Langham fight. It was a famous match that would be long remembered in the history of boxing. It featured Tom Sayers, who was the first heavyweight champion of England, a fighter who went on to fight in the first ever World Championship fight against the American John Camel Heenen. That match ended in a draw following a crowd invasion.

Sayers was well known throughout the land; in his career, he would have sixteen prize fights and lose only one. That one fight was the 1853 Lakenheath fight against another boxing celebrity of the era, Nat Langham. The boxing match is likely to have taken place in the yard of one of the many public houses in the village, and some people having suggested the Bell Hotel could have been the likely venue. If John Trudgett did attend, he would have witnessed Langham gain the upper hand by temporarily blinding his opponent with frequent blows to the eyes. The contest eventually came to an end in the sixty-first round! With Sayers no longer able to see his opponent, Langham could strike him at will. Sayers was still reluctant to give in, and one of his trainers was forced to "throw up the sponge" to signify the end of the contest. Once his eyes had healed, Sayers requested a re-match but Langham announced his retirement from the prize-ring.

As well as a description of the fight, there is a wonderful illustration by an unknown artist who was working for the publication "Famous Fights Past and Present". I have included this image on the Facebook page that accompanies this book, along with contemporary illustrations of Sayers and Langham. I am confident when saying that there will never be another heavyweight bout in Lakenheath.

In 1856, aged twenty-one years, John married Mary Ding at St Ives in Cambridgeshire, with St Ives at that time being in Huntingdonshire. At the time of his marriage, he was still working the windmill with his father. John and his new wife moved into their own home in the village living at number 81 High-street. Although he was no longer living at the mill, he continued to work the windmill with his father. John and Mary soon started a family of their own, an exciting time for the young couple and a new chapter in John's life. A joyous moment in time that would all too quickly turn from joy to the sadness and tragedy that cursed John throughout his life.

It was April 1858, when their first child was born. A baby girl joined their family, whom they named Mary Louisa after her mother. Very soon after the birth of Mary Louisa, Mary fell pregnant with their second child. Tragically they would never become a family of four as they lost their first-born child at just three months old.

Six months after the death of Mary Louisa, John and Mary were parents again. The house that had so suddenly fallen into a silent sadness was once again filled with the sounds of a baby girl as their second child was born. Again, the couple named her after her mother, calling her Mary Ann. They held, cared and loved their second child for six months, until the sadness that seemed to stalk John Trudgett struck once again. The couple were left childless, and the house fell into silence yet again when their second daughter died in July, 1859.

While John and Mary were very raw and fresh from the loss of both of their baby girls, Mary yet again fell pregnant. This time it was John's turn to have the child named after him, when their third child, John, was born. In the 1861 census, the young family were still living in their first family home in the High-street. They were joined on the census entry by John's sister Elizabeth, who was now a nurse. After having lost their first two children, I'm sure that John and Mary would have been grateful for the extra care, attention and reassurance that Elizabeth could offer them and their third child when she came to live with them. Elizabeth could help prevent their baby son, John, being added to the grim statistics that were the child mortality rates in Victorian England. It was as high as 33% for children under five years of age in some areas of England.

There was however, another reason that Elizabeth had been staying with the couple, another reason why John and Mary had required the nursing skills of John's sister. It seemed like a dark curse hovered over John's life, in October 1861, his wife Mary died of Tuberculous, at just twenty-six years of age. The reason for Elizabeth staying with the couple had been to nurse the ill wife of her brother, John. Since the birth of his first child just three years previously, John had now lost his two infant daughters and his wife, leaving him to raise their young son alone.

Ten years later, when the 1871 census was taken, John Trudgett was then living and working at the windmill in Pakenham near Bury St Edmunds, employed by Mary Ann Rampling. The same mill in Pakenham is still a working mill today, 150 years later, having been fully restored in the 1960s.

While John was living away from Lakenheath and working the windmill in Pakenham, John's son (John junior) who was now eleven years old, was learning the family trade himself. John junior was living with his grandfather, James Trudgett (John's father), at the Claypits windmill. James Trudgett was no longer running the mill; John's younger brother, James, was now the miller listed at Claypits. Six years later, in April 1877, James Trudgett died aged twenty-seven years old, and the windmill would now once again be taken over by his father, James Trudgett, until he also died in October of the same year.

The Trudgett family had lost two of the men of the family in just six months—the two men who had been running the family mill. It was a bittersweet year for John Trudgett as he had lost more loved ones, but he did find some happiness that same year when he remarried. Eliza Peachey, a local Lakenheathen, was the daughter of Roper and Rose Peachey who farmed land in the village. Eliza had been working in London for the last twenty years, as a domestic servant and cook. She had now returned back to the village she knew so well from her childhood and married John Trudgett, whom she would have known from growing up in the village. The couple lived at the Claypits mill together, where John was now the miller again following the passing of both his brother and father.

The amazingly unfortunate John once again was struck by tragedy, as in 1882, his only child to survive into adulthood died at twenty-two years of age of acute phthisis. Phthisis, along with consumption, were the medical terms used for tuberculosis. The Victorian disease was also often referred to as "robber of youth", "graveyard cough", "the King's evil", "White death", and "the great white plague". John junior, just like his mother before him, had joined the millions of unfortunate victims of this disease, and his father had lost another child and family member. John Trudgett continued to run the Claypits mill and is listed in the local trade directories in this capacity up until 1892.

With his health deteriorating both physically and mentally, John was unable to work or look after himself. John was forced to enter the workhouse, becoming a resident at the Mildenhall Union in 1893. After entering the workhouse, John was certified as an imbecile. This diagnosis from a medical professional meant that he was not permitted to leave the workhouse, his time there was no longer voluntary and he was instead held captive on medical grounds.

The term imbecile is antiquated terminology, used today as an insult rather than a medical term. The word was used by medical professionals to describe an individual who the Victorian doctor diagnosed as weak minded. The doctor would certify them as an imbecile if they felt the individual was not able to protect himself or herself from moral and mental dangers. Many of the Victorian population who were diagnosed as imbeciles would have been suffering from what we now understand to be dementia. John was showing all the signs of a dementia sufferer when he was certified as an imbecile.

At the age of fifty-eight, John had entered the workhouse, where he would see out his remaining years. John had lived through so many tragic events in his lifetime, losing all three of his children and his first wife, whose lives had been cruelly cut short.

With John in the workhouse and suffering from a decline in his physical and mental health, his wife Eliza left England and travelled to Grahamstown in the Eastern Cape province of South Africa, where her brother Charles Peachey lived. Grahamstown is now called Makhanda. John Trudgett was now without any family and all alone in the world, except for his fellow inmates at the workhouse. It would prove to be a tough and heartbreaking last few years of John's life.

In his first year as a certified imbecile, despite not being permitted to leave the workhouse, John Trudgett escaped and walked to Lakenheath, going back to Claypits windmill, which he still believed that he owned. John Trudgett's sad elopement from the workhouse was reported in the local paper, the Bury Free Press, on April 21st, 1894:

"A very sad occurrence happened on Saturday morning, when the inhabitants [of Lakenheath] were surprised to hear that Mr. John Trudgett, who was removed to Mildenhall Union Workhouse soon after last Michaelmas, had escaped and come back to the windmill on the Common, where he resided for several years. He was seen at 8 a.m. and taken into the millhouse adjoining, where Mr Rutterford now lives, and given some breakfast, for which he was very thankful. He left shortly afterwards, but was seen back again after the absence of over an hour with a wound on his head, which it had been discovered had been struck by one of the mill-sails. P.c. Beech and the Rev F. G. Scrivener were immediately sent for, and he was arrested, having in the meantime made two unsuccessful attempts to cut his throat. He was shortly afterwards removed back to the Mildenhall Workhouse

again."

This event highlighted what a desperately sad existence John was now living. He was suffering from a mental condition that was not yet understood by the medical world, and believing his windmill had been taken from him, he came searching for his home and family. It also demonstrates the well wishes he had from his fellow villagers in Lakenheath, who would have been sad to hear of one of their own falling into such a sad existence.

Having survived being struck by the windmill sails and twice attempting to slit his own throat, John was now back living in the workhouse sharing a room in "Infirmary No.1" with three other men. Those men were: an "imbecile" named John Brown, Richard Rutterford, who was partly blind and deaf, as well as the vicious William Sparke, who had now been an inmate of the workhouse since his release from prison for the attack on his mother. William Sparke had been placed in the room by Mrs Jessup, the Matron, to help keep an eye on the three less physically able men, and to ensure the room was kept clean and to attend the fire.

The final heartbreaking event of John's life took place in 1896, while he was still suffering from delusions that the Claypits windmill rightfully belonged to him. John would often try to escape so that he could get back to Lakenheath, in the hope of reclaiming his mill as he had done two years previously in an incident where he had been fortunate not to die.

On the night of Monday, 2nd March, 1896, John attempted several times to get out of his bed and leave the workhouse. William Sparke became increasingly annoyed with his fellow roommate's disruptive behaviour, and an incident then occurred between the men which left John Trudgett in a bloody condition and fighting for his life.

Charles Jessup, the workhouse master, met his wife Sarah in the men's room at 10 a.m. on the Tuesday morning. Sarah Jessup called her husband over and drew his attention to John Trudgett. In the court case that followed the attack, Sarah Jessup gave the following account of how she had found John Trudgett, "He had been ill-treated, his face covered in bruises, there were blood stains on his face, he was pulse less and in a state of collapse". On entering the room, Sarah Jessup had also found an iron poker on the floor. Sarah explained that this was against the rules, and the men in this room had been banned from having an iron poker, as the "old men" would quarrel and use it against each other.

On discovering John Trudgett in a bloody state, Charles Jessup asked William Sparke what had happened. At that time, William Sparke denied hitting John, instead his response was that "John had been rolling about all night and knocking himself against the bedstead." Before the master and matron had come to the room, a fellow inmate named Fred Barret had already entered the room to bring the four men their breakfast, and on entering, he noticed John Trudgett sitting on the side of his bed, partly dressed, his left eye black and unable to speak. Barret asked William Sparke if he fell out of bed at which point William told him "No, I hit him".

Odden Frederic Read, the chairman of the Board of Guardians, heard about this and attended the workhouse on the Tuesday evening; he visited Trudgett, who was in a semi-conscious condition. Odden Read also asked William Sparke what had happened that night, to which the response was, "The old man was very troublesome last night and kept getting out of bed; I tried to put him back, and he fell down and did it himself."

Odden Read told William Sparke that he did not find the explanation sufficient to account for the condition of Trudgett.

Sparke then said "I did hit him; I gave him a clout over the head".

The medical officer, Dr. Aldrich, saw John Trudgett between 10 a.m. and 11 a.m., after he was discovered by the Master and Matron. Dr. Aldrich was asked to describe the condition in which he found John Trudgett when he arrived, "I found him in a state of collapse. He had contusions about the face and head and appeared to be dying". Trudgett did eventually die five days after the attack, bringing to an end what appears to have been a life of sorrow.

Dr. Aldrich, the medical officer, carried out a post mortem on John Trudgett and found an abrasion three inches long on his back and on the inner side of the left shoulder blade. This appeared to be a recent injury, caused within a week of his death. The body was extremely emaciated and both lungs were intensely congested. Dr. Aldrich attributed the death to shock to the system, the result from the injuries. Dr. Aldrich told the jury he did not think the injuries were caused by a man's hand or fist, but a stick half a yard long and 5/8" thick would be more likely to have caused the injuries. This sounds very much like another iron poker attack to me!

William Sparke was committed to trial for the manslaughter of John Trudgett. Despite Dr. Aldrich giving evidence that he believed the death was caused by shock from injury inflicted that night, injuries that could not have been self-inflicted, and despite William Sparke's admission to the court that he had hit John Trudgett, the jury found William Sparke not guilty of man-slaughter.

I wonder if the court was aware of William's previous attack on his mother, also with an iron poker. It seemed that the description of the injury to John Trudgett's back fitted perfectly with the iron poker that Sarah Jessup had found on the floor of the room that morning. I was obviously not there at the time, but having read all the newspaper reports in detail and having played a lot of Cluedo, I believe this was the blacksmith, in the infirmary, with the iron poker!

John Trudgett did not have a valid Will, so a Grant of Administration was granted to his wife Eliza. A Grant of Administration is a legal document used when a valid Will is not left, and it does not consider the wishes of the deceased, so it is unknown how John would have wished for his estate to be distributed.

Eliza never returned from South Africa and continued to live in Grahamstown right up until her death in 1916. Her death certificate lists the cause of death as "Cancer" and duration of illness as "Years".

CHAPTER NINE

James Munson 1827 – 1898

James Munson led an unremarkable life, leaving behind very little evidence he ever walked this earth. A basket weaver from the tiny village of Beck Row, he left his tiny village to live amongst a few people in the recently drained fenlands. Everyone has a story to tell, and even in what seems the most mundane of existences, there are tales to be told. This chapter is about the unremarkable life of a basket weaver.

James Munson was born in 1827 in Beck Row, a small village just a few miles from Mildenhall. James had three siblings, brothers Silvanis and Elias and Easter, a younger sister. Their parents were James Munson (Senior) and Phillis Munson (nee Smith), and they were a family who made their living selling baskets in the local area.

Beck Row is the village where I too grew up as a child, and even in my lifetime, the village has changed from a small community with a local village shop at its heart to what is now essentially a town with modern housing estates rapidly popping up, squeezed into every inch of land possible, but still with only a village shop to service them. The major expansion of Beck Row followed the construction of Mildenhall Airbase between Mildenhall and Beck Row in 1934. The airbase cut off the main route from Mildenhall to the small village, and a new road now circumnavigates the Base perimeter fence. During World War II, the Base was under RAF Bomber command and was used for operation combat missions. The Australian pilot Ron Middleton, who was a posthumous recipient of the Victoria Cross, was based here and is buried in the graveyard at St John's church. In the 1950s, the American Air Force became tenants of the airbase and have remained ever since. Beck Row expanded at a fast rate to house the American servicemen, and this expansion has continued ever since, particularly so in the last twenty years.

During James Munson's lifetime, Beck Row was not easily accessible as there were only two ways to enter the village, the first being to travel down Folly-road in Mildenhall, continuing towards Beck Row with large open fields on either side. One would eventually meet up with the street in Beck Row, the route now cut off by Mildenhall Airbase, which has since been built over the large open fields. The second option would be to travel via West Row following Hurdle Drove and Pollards lane before it opened into agricultural land, eventually becoming a small sandy track, entering Beck Row and passing a few isolated cottages and the village pond, before arriving at The Bird in Hand public house. The road that now links Beck Row and West Row was not built until 1942.

Beck Row is a village James Munson would now struggle to recognise. It does, however, have nineteen hectares of land that are now a protected ancient medieval wood pasture. It contains over two hundred oaks, some of which may be up to one thousand years old, scattered around undulating grass pastures formed in the last ice age. Used by previous generations to both graze their sheep and harvest the precious oak wood, anyone from Beck Row, past or present, would instantly recognise the unique landscape. As a young boy growing up in the village, I climbed many of the ancient oak trees, placing my hands and feet on the protruding lumps and crevices caused by years of pollarding, the very same hand and foot holes that a young James Munson would have discovered as he explored the ancient landscape. I think it is partly for this reason that I feel a connection with James Munson and probably why I spent hours researching what seemed from the outset a fairly unremarkable life.

James Munson was a basket weaver; a skill he had been taught by his father, who was also a basket weaver. The basket weaving trade had exploded in the Victorian era as the industrial revolution meant that baskets were in high demand for use in factories and to store or transport goods. In the early 1800s, over three thousand acres of willows had been planted to supply the basket weaving trade.

The Munsons not only made baskets but any item that required weaving, including bee hives and eel traps. The Victorian beehive, which was known as a skep, was essentially an upturned straw basket under which bees would form their honeycomb. The Victorian era saw a rise in beekeeping, and many people started to keep bees not just for honey production but also science. Charles Darwin kept bees in his garden at Down House, and these bees helped Darwin formulate his theories on evolution. An important tradition for Victorian beekeepers was "telling it to the bees", and important events in the beekeepers' lives such as births, marriages or deaths were told to the bees. If the bees were not informed, or "put into mourning", it was believed that the bees would leave or stop producing honey.

On 9th May, 1885, James Munson advertised his beehives for sale in the local paper, the Bury Free Press:

GOOD Strong-made **BEEHIVES** at 1s each. —
Apply to JAMES MUNSON, Beehive-maker,
Beck-Row, Mildenhall, Suffolk

Munson was selling his beehives for 1s each, which is the equivalent of about £15 each today. It's interesting that the advertisement doesn't give any details of where to find James Munson other than the village where he lived. I like to think people would just have to turn up in Beck Row and walk around asking for James Munson, beehive maker!

In the 1841 census, fourteen-year-old James was living with his parents in Sandy Hill, Beck Row, along with his siblings Silvanis, Elias and sister Easter. Having grown up in Beck Row myself, I had never heard of Sandy Hill, and it definitely does not exist today and is not labelled on any maps from the time. I have asked older residents of Beck Row if they recall the street name or area, but have had no luck; it seems to be a forgotten street name. Having pieced clues together from several census records, I believe Sandy Hill was the previous name for what we now know as "The Street", changing its name sometime between 1881 and 1891.

The 1851 census record shows that James Munson Snr, James and his brother Elias, are all listed as basket makers, still living in Beck Row, along with Phillis and Easter. James' elder brother, Silvanis, is a sad omission from this census, having passed away the previous year at just twenty-three years of age. The Munsons must have had a decent basket weaving business, with the three men producing a large number of the baskets required by the locals.

James moved out of the family home in 1857, after marrying a local Mildenhall girl, Eliza Cox, at St Mary's Church in Mildenhall. The couple had their only child two years later, when their daughter Elizabeth was born. The young family lived together in Burnt Fen, where James was an agricultural labourer. Labouring now seemed to be his main source of income, with maybe basket weaving as a side business.

Burnt Fen is an area of drained fenland between Beck Row and Ely that lies below sea level. It is prime agricultural land that is totally dependent on pumping stations to stop the land from flooding. Burnt Fen, even today, is very sparsely populated. At the time the Munsons lived there, they were one of only nine households living in Burnt fen. ,

For centuries there had been attempts to drain the fens, which always met with fierce opposition by locals who made their living fishing and wildfowling the water. In the 1630s, a major attempt to drain the fens was sabotaged by fenmen who called themselves the Fen Tigers. The venture was successful, despite the Fen Tigers' attempts of sabotage. For a few decades, the land was farmed, until the end of the century, when it was once again below water. The peat as it dried out was sinking further and further below sea level, before permanently flooding again.

It was only in the 1820s, just thirty years before James and Eliza moved to Burnt Fen, that the area was successfully drained. The drainage attempts had yet again been met by local outrage and sabotage, but this time long-term success was achieved by using steam engines to keep the water constantly pumped away from the land. During James Munson's lifetime, Burnt Fen was kept from flooding by pumping carried out by two steam engines, which were manufactured by Boulton and Watt, and located in the river Lark and Little Ouse.

In 1871, James and Eliza were still living and working in the fens with their daughter, Elizabeth. Also living with them was their eight-year-old niece, Charlotte (Lottie) Cox. Lottie would have been a welcome playmate for their only child, Elizabeth, who would have had very few other children to play with whilst living out in the fens.

Lottie had previously been living with her brothers, sisters and parents in Methwold, where she had been born. The rest of her family remained in Methwold while she lived with her aunt and uncle in the fens.

Lottie's younger brother was born in 1874 and named after the former American president, George Washington. Her brother, George Washington Cox, is testimony to her parents' desire to emigrate to America for a better life. They wanted to be part of the American dream — an idea that appealed to 3,5000,000 Britons who emigrated to America between 1820 and 1930. In 1883, nine years after the birth of her brother, George Washington, Charlotte along with her parents, brothers, sisters and future husband all set off to start a new life in America. Lottie discovered her new life in New York. I could not think of any place on earth that would contrast with her previous home of Burnt Fen as much as did New York — a melting pot of different cultures, full of tall skyscrapers. Even in Lottie's lifetime, the contrast with the flat sparse uninhabited land of the Fens must have been remarkable for her.

James and Eliza Munson did not buy into the American dream, instead they moved to Eriswell, another Suffolk village on the outskirts of Lakenheath. James Munson moved to Eriswell in order to work as a farm bailiff. This was an important position working for the landowner, as he would need to ensure tenant farmers on the land kept the farms in good order and paid their rent on time. He was the middleman between the tenant farmers and landowner.

It was while living in Eriswell that James tragically lost both his wife and his only child, as in April 1877, his 18-year-old daughter, Elizabeth, passed away, followed about twelve months later by her mother, Eliza. In the Victorian era, widows and widowers were created far too often and far too young; it makes one appreciate the world in which we live today, where we have eradicated many of the diseases that stalked the Victorian population and have now discovered medicines that can cure illnesses that just a few decades previous could be a death sentence. As recently as the 1930s, my great-grandmother died aged in her thirties of pneumonia. Ten years into the future, she would have been given antibiotics and lived to see her children and grandchildren grow into adulthood.

James Munson, having recently become a widower, decided to

downsize and move away from Eriswell, back to Beck Row—the village where he was born and where he would presumably have family support. In the same month that his wife Eliza died, the following advertisement was placed on Saturday 12th October, 1878, in the Bury Free Press, as James was selling up and moving on:

ERISWELL, NEAR MILDENHALL
ALL THE NEAT
HOUSEHOLD FURNITURE

INCLUDING 3 feather beds, mattresses, bedding,
marble-top and other washstands, dressing tables,
&c. linen, mahogony bureau, American 8 day and
other clocks, mahogony-framed couch, hollow-seat and
easy chairs, mahogony and other tables, kitchen and
culinary requisites, which

JOHN W. WILLIAMS

Is instructed by Mr. JAMES MUNSON (who is
declining housekeeping) to Sell by Auction, on
FRIDAY, October 18th, 1878, at One o clock
punctually.

Catalogues posted free on application to the Auctioneer .

The furniture was advertised for sale due to "declining housekeeping"; this being a common phrase used by auctioneers towards the end of the 19th century. It did not mean that James did not want to clean or tidy his house or was unable to do so, but that he no longer needed these items. The equivalent term today would be "downsizing".

James Munson moved to 25 Sandy Hill, Beck Row, where he lived a lonely life on his own. In the 1881 census, James was again listed as a basket maker, and we know that in 1885, he was advertising his skills as a bee hive maker. It was evident that he was again making his living using the skills passed down to him by his father. Ten years later, in the 1891 census, we still find James Munson living on his own in the same small cottage and still working as a basket maker, although the address was now referred to as "High Street".

On March 11, 1898, the final days of James Munson's life were starting to unfold. As he was now in his seventies and suffering from bronchitis, he entered himself into the workhouse infirmary for treatment. Bronchitis was second only to consumption (tuberculosis) in the Victorian era as a cause of death.

The treatment for bronchitis, like many treatments in the nineteenth century, was not particularly helpful. Patients were taken away from polluted air sources, which I agree, was a good measure! However, this was followed by such treatments as inhalation of tobacco fumes, tincture of cannabis (dissolved in alcohol), opium in various forms, counter pressure provided by plasters and bandages, as well as various ointments. Despite the questionable treatments available at the time, James Munson was nursed back to health by the medical staff at the workhouse.

James remained convalescing at the workhouse and was still present a month later in April, 1898, when one Sunday afternoon he took a walk around the grounds. He walked down the path that led to the pigsty, which was some distance from any other buildings. A fellow inmate named Alfred Gaul walked alongside him. As they reached the pigsty, Alfred turned right, leaving James Munson standing at the pigsty on his own. As Alfred walked away from James, he heard him shout out, "Good day, I don't think I shall see you anymore." Alfred replied with, "Good day", and carried on his way. These would be the last words spoken by James Munson.

At half past four, another inmate named James Curtis, went to feed the pigs and found James Munson laying on his back with his head lifted off the ground. There was a boot lace around his neck which was tied to the top of some iron fencing. James Curtis cut Munson down and fetched Charles Jessup. He came immediately and found the deceased laying on the floor "quite dead, with two shoelaces around his neck".

Dr. Geoffrey Hudson, the medical officer who had previously attended James Munson at the infirmary said he considered Munson was "of weak intellect, but not lunatic nor imbecile and did not require any special attention". At the inquest into James Munson's death, the jury returned a verdict of "suicide by temporary insanity" and expressed the opinion that no blame was attached to any of the officials at the workhouse.

CHAPTER TEN

Rachel Andrews 1868 – 1939

Rachel Andrews was a lady who made poor choices in life, resulting in her descent into a petty criminal. Stealing low value items of clothing in the dead of the night, She was twice imprisoned for her petty thefts. She lost her whole family and lived a lonely existence without them. Was she a blameless victim of circumstances, oppressed by the Victorian system which kept the rich wealthy and the poor destitute, or was she to blame for her own poor decisions which led to her lonely existence as a Victorian pauper?

Rachel Andrews was one of five children born to parents Hannah and Charles Andrews, Charles being a shoe maker from Beck Row. The Andrews lived next door to the Munsons about whom we read in the previous chapter, although in 1868 when Rachel was born only James Munson senior was left living at this address in Sandy Hill, having become a widower four years previously.

Rachel Andrews became part of the Ingle family in 1892, when she married William Ingle. The Ingle family were a well known working class family from West Row, appearing regularly in the local paper for misdemeanors that we would not consider newsworthy today. Swearing in public and being drunk on the streets were common crimes for members of the Ingle family. The Victorians had strict moral beliefs, and swearing in public was not acceptable. Neither was being drunk in public and, in fact, the 1872 Licensing Act also forbade being drunk on licensed premises. Middle and upper class men would swear in private and it was also acceptable to swear amongst a group of men. "Let's retire to the drawing room for some whiskey and F-bombs". In Victorian England, if you were born poor, you died poor, and the lower classes knew this; life was hard for the poor and they would swear when they bloody wanted to swear.

Rachel and William Ingle lived in Beck Row after their marriage, and their family grew in 1894 when their first child was born, a boy they named George William; a boy who would grow up to become a soldier and a hero. Another baby boy followed in 1895 when Peter was born, followed a year later in 1896 by the birth of Sarah. The yearly event of child birth gave way to the death of a child in 1897, when Peter died at just two years old. Their youngest and last child was Blanche in 1899.

Something went horribly wrong for the Ingles as William appears to have abandoned his family shortly after the birth of Blanche. In 1901, without the financial support of her husband, Rachel admitted herself and her two young girls into the workhouse, where they can be seen on the 1901 census listed as paupers.

Entering the workhouse with young children was the last resort of a single desperate woman. Often, if a family was abandoned, the wife would claim to be a widow rather than admit that her husband had left her, but this was not the case with Rachel who was listed as being married when she entered the workhouse. Entering the workhouse was always a last resort for young families who would be split and sent to separate segregated areas of the house. If it was the only option you had to feed and shelter your children, then you can understand why Rachel would have entered with her girls. Sarah and Blanche were both under seven at the time of admittance, and if it was deemed "expedient", the workhouse was permitted to house children of this age with their mother, sharing her bed. I like to imagine this is what happened to Rachel and her girls, with Rachel comforting their sobs at night, rather than the young girls having only each other for comfort in this "Victorian prison".

The young girls' father, William, and older brother, George William, did not join them in the workhouse. Seven year old George William was instead living with his grandparents, Thomas and Elizabeth Ingle in West Row, listed as their "son", he had been given the opportunity to escape life in the workhouse and had shelter and food with his loving grandparents.

William Ingle has so far evaded the eyes of history. I have found no definite record of where the man had gone in 1901. It was against the law for him to enter his family into the workhouse without admitting himself as well, so he either abandoned his family or possibly was being held at His Majesty's pleasure. However, prison seems an unlikely whereabouts for William as there are no reports in the local papers of his conviction and he doesn't appear on the census records for any of the local prisons. Rachel Ingle is listed as being married on her census record taken at the workhouse in April 1901.

There is possibly a clue as to why William Ingle left his wife and family, which comes in the form of a strange advertisement printed in the Bury Free Press on 8th June 1895. Tucked away amongst advertisements for umbrellas, coals, marquees and various other items for sale there is an announcement from Ingle and another notice from H.J. Ingle, Tobacconist, who stated that the following Public Notice did not refer to him

"NOTICE, that W. Ingle will not be responsible
for any debts contracted by Mrs. Ingle after this
date. May 31 1895"

This advertisement, although it seems odd to us now, was a fairly common occurrence in local papers throughout the country. If a couple split, then the husband often took out an announcement in the local paper to ensure no future debts came his way. The Complete English Lawyer, a book published in 1820, was a general reference book for the public that covered all aspects of the law, taxes and legal processes at the time of its publication. It gave details of laws and taxes to which the Victorians were subject and the penalties which they would expect to receive if those laws were broken. It detailed the poor laws and parish settlement, matrimonial, libel, bankruptcy, Wills and many, many other subjects. In this book the following passage can be found, which explains why men who had split from their wife would take out such an advert.

*"With respect to the husband's liability for his wife's contracts it may be observed in general, that a husband being bound to provide his wife with necessaries, if she contract debts for them, he is answerable, **unless he gave express notice** to the tradesman not to trust her... ...If the wife with consent of her husband, live apart from him, and has separate maintenance, and contract debts*

*for necessaries, it is incumbent on the husband to shew that the tradesman **had notice of the separate maintenance"***

Rachel gave birth to her two girls Sarah and Blanche and son Peter, after the date of the advertisement, who are recorded as having the surname Ingle, so it's possible that William and Rachel split in 1895 and that he's not the father of the children, but that she used the name Ingle for her children to avoid the stigma of having illegitimate children.

William Ingle appears again in 1905, when he marries his second wife, Emma Burgess, in Bromley, before the couple emigrated to Canada in 1907. William had another two children with his second wife, those being George (named after William's grandfather and also the name of his son from his first marriage) and a girl named Elizabeth after William's mother. William used the name John on Canadian census records, but when his daughter Elizabeth married, he was again recorded as William. In 1937, when he died in Canada, thirty years after he arrived there, his death certificate again refers to him as William, born in England to parents Elizabeth and Thomas Ingle, the parents to whom he had been born in West Row. There is no doubt that this is the same William Ingle who left his wife and children in the workhouse and started a new life in Canada.

Back in the workhouse, Rachel was having a torrid time. Her younger daughter, Blanche, had fallen ill, which led to the death of the infant child. Blanche passed away in the workhouse in 1902. The death certificate for Blanche Ingle has the cause of death listed as Tabes mesenterica, tuberculosis meningitis, and convulsions. Tabes mesenterica, we now understand, was caused by bovine TB which could flourish in the bacteria friendly environment of sour milk. Rachel had been feeding Blanche on either cows' milk or formula (which was cows' milk with the addition of wheat, malt flour, and potassium bicarbonate). Watching the poor three-year-old Blanche waste away whilst her poor frail body was in convulsions must have been horrendous for Rachel.

Bottle feeding had soared in popularity in the Victorian era. The bottle itself was a highly dangerous design; a glass bottle with a rubber feeding tube that could not easily be cleaned. The "go to" advice for Victorian wives was Mrs. Beeton's Book for Household Management. In this book Mrs. Beeton recommends cleaning the rubber tube of babies' bottles every two to three weeks. Some deadly advice!

If the bottle itself was not dangerous enough, then the milk was just as dangerous if not more so. Cows' milk was unpasteurised at this time, and refrigeration was not available to keep the milk fresh. The milk was generally very unhygienically produced and moved around, being ladled out of buckets or carried around the streets in jugs, all this meaning that milk had a very short shelf life before it would become fatally dangerous for humans to drink. Mrs. Beeton had yet more advice for the British public in her famous book, this time for spoilt milk, to which she recommended adding boracic acid to the milk to remove the sour taste and smell. "Quite a harmless addition" she wrote. Mrs. Beeton was very wrong on this one, as the sour milk harboured bovine TB, and infant mortality rate soared for children who were fed by a bottle. Being fed on cows' milk placed the child at high risk of contracting tuberculosis as well as many other diseases. Approximately 500,000 children died between 1850 and 1950 from tuberculosis transmitted to them through the milk. This killer was only brought under control as milk became increasingly pasteurised in the 1930s and 1940s.

Mrs. Beeton's book, written by Isabella Beeton, was first published in 1861 and was immensely popular. Selling over two million copies by 1868, it remained popular well into the twentieth century, and is still referenced and sold today as one of the most iconic books of the Victorian era. It was, however, written by a twenty-one year old Isabella who may possibly have never cooked before, and offered some odd advice (see the aforementioned poor milk advice) and ideas on cooking.

Mrs. Beeton's Household Management is responsible for a British tradition of tasteless and over-boiled vegetables, which lasted well into the 1980s, as mothers and wives were warned by Mrs. Beeton's book that "Vegetables that are cooked in a raw state are apt to ferment in the stomach". Other oddities in her book include boiling pasta for an hour and forty-five minutes! She described the taste of mangoes as like turpentine, lobsters as indigestible, garlic as offensive, potatoes "suspicious; a great many are narcotic, and many are deleterious" and cheese could only be consumed by sedentary people. She also had a very conflicting view on the humble tomato, seemingly undecided if they were an amazingly wholesome fruit or so disagreeable that they would cause you to vomit just from their smell. The passage reproduced below from her book is a very odd piece of writing where her view on the tomato changes as you read down the page.

"(The tomato's) flavour stimulates the appetite, and is almost universally approved. The tomato is a wholesome fruit, and digests easily. ...it has been found to contain a particular acid, a volatile oil, a brown, very fragrant extracto-resinous matter, a vegeto-mineral matter, muco-saccharine, some salts, and, in all probability, an alkaloid. The whole plant has a disagreeable odour, and its juice, subjected to the action of the fire, emits a vapour so powerful as to cause vertigo and vomiting."

Rachel left the workhouse and continued to live in Beck Row, working as a domestic servant. Her daughter Sarah moved in with her grandparents, Hannah and Christopher Fincham (Rachel's mother and stepfather), who also lived in Beck Row. In the 1911 census, thirteen year old Sarah is listed as being at school. Beck Row school was built in 1877, and there were separate doors and playgrounds for the girls and boys. It could accommodate one hundred children. I also attended Beck Row school as a young lad and I can distinctly remember the stones carved with "Boys" and "Girls" in the original archways of the old building. A few years ago, I was given permission to metal detect the school fields at Beck Row. I found over one hundred coins in one day. Many of them were dated to a time Sarah would have been at the school, so I may have found a coin dropped by Sarah.

In the 1911 census, Rachel Ingle is listed at an address in Great Saxham near Bury St Edmunds, where she was working as a housekeeper for Ernest Crouch, a twenty-nine-year-old widower and his two young sons. Rachel is listed as a widow herself, although in reality her husband had not died but had left and started a new life in Canada. It was quite common for a deserted wife to claim to be a widow, as divorce was almost impossible unless you were rich. In fact, up until the late 1870s, only around three hundred divorces in England had ever been granted. This resulted in many couples separating and maybe starting a new life in a bigamous marriage. There was also a common belief among the lower classes that there was a seven year law where, if a husband or wife was overseas or missing for this period of time, he or she could be presumed dead and a remarriage or declaring yourself a widow or widower was possible.

In fact, a court order declaring the person to be dead was needed, but as most people were unaware of this, many more bigamous marriages took place in the nineteenth century than we would assume.

Rachel's son, George William Ingle, had been raised by his grandparents, Thomas and Elizabeth Ingle, as their own son. Why they saved him from a life of poverty with his mother but not his younger sisters is not known. Perhaps they felt that because the girls were younger and needed their mother. Perhaps they had no room for all three children, or just maybe they did not believe that the girls were the children of their son. In the 1911 census Thomas and Elizabeth Ingle list themselves as having had seven children, and as I have only found birth records for 6 children for Thomas and Elizabeth, it seems that they included their grandson as a son.

George William Ingle, now grown up, had left his grandparents' home and joined the Army. In the 1911 census he was stationed at the Gibralter Barracks in Bury St. Edmunds in Out Risbeygate Street. The Barracks still stand today, a very impressive Victorian building that dominates the street, next to the West Suffolk College as one enters Bury St Edmunds.

Without her husband or children, Rachel's life was miserable. Struggling to make ends meet, she was forced to take drastic action, even for basic needs such as clothing, and so was forced to steal. In 1913, Rachel was arrested for stealing clothes; not just one incident but on four different occasions. If Rachel had been caught stealing four times, I'm sure there would have been many more incidents of theft for which she was never caught. If she was stealing clothes, it is possible that she would have also been forced to steal food to survive. Rachel's crime spree was centered around the Norwich area, so she must have been living or working in this area at the time.

Her crimes, detailed below, have been taken from her trial on 7th January 1914 and reported in the Lowestoft Journal on Saturday 10th January 1914:

> "...Feloniously stolen two sheets, of the goods of Charlotte Hipkin, at Bramerton, on the November 8th.;
> two aprons, one undervest, and one night dress, of the goods of Elizabeth Moore, at Kriby Bedon, on the 6th November .;
> one shirt, two blouses and one pair of knickers, of the goods of Agnes Chamberlain, at Swainsthorpe, on November 13th;

and one pair of boots, of the goods of Walter Rix, at Bramerton, between 6th and 10th November last [1913]."

Rachel pleaded guilty to the first three offences and was found guilty and sentenced on each indictment to "three months hard labour (to be served concurrently)". Hard labour was introduced to prisons in 1877. It was back-breaking and demoralising work, with the intention of reforming the convict and deterring others from crime. The soul-destroying hard labour was finally abolished in 1948.

Rachel could look forward to between six to ten hours hard labour each day; the crank, capstan, shot-drill and stone-breaking were all acceptable types of hard labour, but the most dreaded was the treadmill. No one could claim prisons were soft during this period.

Hard labour was designed to deter the prisoner from carrying out further crimes on their release, but sadly this was not successful in the case of Rachel Ingle. Even after her demoralising punishment of hard labour, she was still desperate enough to steal.

On 10th April 1915, she was again in the local press. This time the Lynn News & County Press detailed her theft of a nightdress and other items in East Winch, near Kings Lynn.

*"**Theft at East Winch** – Rachel Ingle, housekeeper, Mildenhall, Suffolk, was charged on remand with stealing a lady's nightdress, a twill sheet and a pair of wool stockings, on March 23 or 24, value 8s. P.C. Marshall said he saw the articles in the house one evening. Next morning, he saw defendant on the road at 2.15am, and he spoke to her for being out at that time. She said that a strange man was after her. She ran away and threw down the missing articles. - Defendant pleaded guilty and elected to be tried by the magistrates. - The Chairman said this was not the first time the defendant had been charged for larceny, and she would go to prison for 6 weeks with hard labour."*

While Rachel was serving her second sentence of hard labour, her daughter Sarah passed away. At the time of her death, she had still been living with her grandparents in Beck Row. Her death certificate reveals that she was yet another victim of the dreaded Victorian plague "consumption". Sarah died of pulmonary consumption; this being tuberculosis infection of the lungs. She passed away on the 3rd May 1915, after cardiac failure at the age of seventeen.

Sarah's grandmother, Hannah, had been present at the death and is recorded on the death certificate as the informant. Hannah has placed her "mark" i.e. a cross in the box, where the registrar has then written next to this cross "the mark of Hannah Fincham, grandmother, present at death, Beck Row". In the 1800s when Sarah's grandmother Hannah was a child growing up, less than half the female population could read and write, and only 60% of the male population. It seems odd to us now that Hannah would not even be able to write her own name, but this was very common for a lady of Hannah's age at the turn of the century.

Before 1870, when the Education Act was introduced, only 50% of children in the U.K. had access to education, but with the 1870 Act local by-laws could now make it compulsory for 5–13 year old children to attend school. They could, however, leave at the age of ten if the local board felt they had reached the required level of education. In 1876, there were to be major changes when the Sandon Act imposed a legal duty for parents to send their children to school, and again in 1891, when the Elementary Education Act provided free education for children. Children who worked had to have a certificate to show that they attended a school up to the age of ten and had reached the required level of education. Employers could be penalised if they employed children who did not have this certificate. The Victorians had moved education towards the system we know today, and it was in this period in history that many of our local primary schools in the area were built.

Following the death of her daughter Sarah, Rachel only had one surviving child, George William. He was now fighting in the First World War with the 4th Hussars, the same regiment in which Winston Churchill had served before him.

In May 1915, while his mother was doing hard labour for her continued poor conduct, George William was awarded the Distinguished Conduct Medal. Fighting on the front line, the 4th Hussars were under heavy attack. George William's commanding officer was seriously wounded, lying on the ground in No Man's Land and unable to move. Despite being wounded himself, George procured a wheelbarrow from a nearby farm to rescue the officer.

George William Ingle dodged bullets and shells to pull the officer into the wheelbarrow before he wheeled him back to safety, despite being under very heavy enemy fire the whole time. Once back to safety, George William collapsed from loss of blood and was taken to the base hospital to recover. While recovering in hospital Private

George William Ingle received a letter from his commanding officer:

"I was very glad to see in today's paper that you have been awarded the D.C.M for the plucky way you brought Lieut. Radclyffe back to the dressing station, although you were suffering a great deal yourself. I feel proud to have been in command of such men, and hope you will continue to do as well as you have done in the past and manage to escape the bullets, etc. I myself am quite fit again now and ready to return to the regiment any time, when I hope I will be put in command of the old 4th troop again. Remember me to any of the old troop that are with you

Yours Truly C.B Ainslie"

George William Ingle also received a letter from Lieutenant Radclyffe, the officer whose life he saved. As well as the letter, Radclyffe also sent a gift of a wrist watch inscribed:

"No. 7028, Private George Ingle
from Lieutenant Radclyffe. 4th Hussars
May 2nd 1915. Wieltje"

The letter that accompanied the wrist watch read:

"I am sending you a watch as a small memento of the plucky way you helped to carry me back when I was wounded, in spite of being wounded yourself. I hope you are quite fit and do not feel any ill effect of your wound"

It was certainly a whirlwind couple of months for the Ingle family; the death of Sarah Ingle, William George's D.C.M. and Rachel's imprisonment all occurring at the same time.

After a spell in the base hospital, George William Ingle returned to the front line with his regiment, being promoted to Lance Corporal Ingle.

On 23rd March 1918, Rachel lost her last remaining child when George William Ingle was killed in action. On this day, the 4th Hussars were trying to hold back the Germans near Mennessis (south of Saint Quentin), on the third day of the German Spring offensive. They had seven men killed, one of them being Lance Corporal George Ingle.

I've been amazed how often during the research of the workhouse that it's led me to the Mildenhall War Memorial, and yet again I find myself looking at the Mildenhall Memorial where George Ingle was commemorated. His name was, however, later removed at the time that West Row erected their own monument. The removal of his name seems totally unnecessary, as I'm sure he could have been commemorated on two memorials without any issue.

George Ingle's name being removed from the Mildenhall Monument is just one incident of a poorly managed monument to our local war heroes. It seems very odd behavior to treat fallen soldiers the way local authorities in Mildenhall have done over the years.

The bizarre management of this monument seems to date back to the very first unveiling of the monument. Some of the poor decisions are listed below.

- In October 1920, the monument was unveiled three weeks early by a member of the public, as a protest over delay of an Official Ceremony.

- Originally unveiled with one hundred and five names, a further six were added in 1921, including Augustus Jessup (about whom we learnt from a previous chapter).

- The names were then reduced to eighty-six, presumably as the villages erected their own monuments. Again this makes little sense as several men from surrounding villages are still listed. Why remove them? Would it matter if they are remembered in their village as well as the nearby town?

- The names of F. J. Balls and W. Jaggard were later put back onto the monument.

- R. Wells was listed twice i.e. as Lance Corporal Wells and also Corporal Wells. Corporal Wells was removed when names were reduced to eighty-six, but it is not clear if this was due to a duplication.

- Soldier J. Mizen was actually J. Fuller. The name J. Mizen was removed but J. Mizen or J. Fuller do not appear on any of the other local monuments. This man now seems forgotten.

- It also seems a man was commemorated who actually lived into the 1950s .

- The monument originally had a lengthy ninety word dedication which was reduced at a later date to a thirty-five word dedication.

- In 1946, the Parish Council was to remove the statue of the soldier from the monument, but it was met with a strong protest from the British Legion. Fortunately, the British Legion won and the soldier remained. This was reported in the Bury Free Press at the time. There was no obvious reason to remove the soldier and it seems very odd the Parish Council were going to do this.

- In recent times, vandals broke the soldier's gun. This was repaired in a very poor way, and the gun sights are now underneath the weapon, and remain this way today.

As a monument dedicated to the memory of local soldiers killed in action, some of the decisions over the years seem very odd and ill-thought, from the time it was unveiled up to the recent poorly repaired rifle.

George William listed his grandmother Hannah Andrews (Rachel's Mother) as his sole legatee on his Army records. This is surprising as his other grandmother, Elizabeth Ingle, was still alive at this stage and had brought him up as her own. It is, however, no surprise that he did not list his mother. When he died, the Army paid his grandmother £71 (value about £900 today), which was a decent sum of money. It would have bought his mother several nightdresses of which she seemed fond. Rachel Ingle claimed his Army Dependents Pension and was listed on his pension card in 1920. She made sure she did not miss out on some of the money to which she felt entitled.

Rachel Ingle's hard life came to an end in January 1939, after losing all four of her children at a young age, admitting herself into the workhouse, being left by her husband and twice being imprisoned with hard labour, she could finally be at peace. She passed away in Newmarket, aged 71 years.

CHAPTER ELEVEN

Samuel Ingle 1868 – 1949

Samuel Ingle was not a little boy with whom you wanted to play as a child, and not the man with whom you wanted to have a drink as an adult. Samuel was full of violence from a young age, and when the red mist descended, he attacked. He didn't care who they were, and he had no respect for any form of authority—they were getting a slap or a kick as well. In 1915, Samuel Ingle found himself in the Mildenhall Union Workhouse, and wherever Samuel went, violence followed! The workhouse would be no different.

Samuel Ingle was born in West Row in 1868, to parents Thomas and Harriet Ingle. Born into a large family, he was one of fourteen siblings. Maybe it was establishing his place in the pecking order of this large family that created Samuel's need to resort to violence. Samuel Ingle was actually second cousin to William Ingle, the eloping husband of Rachel from the previous chapter. The Ingles were certainly a large tribe in West Row. I've lived two miles down the road from this village for the last forty years, and I can't think of anyone with that surname left in the village.

I have three children myself, who are my absolute world, (and funnily, one of my boys is also named Samuel), but they are very testing. Sometimes it feels like I have a mini mutiny on my hands, as they gang up on me and my wife to get their own way. Naked protests, tears, sulking, screaming and arguing are the go-to methods for our children, (luckily not the violence Samuel Ingle resorted to), so our house is pure pandemonium at times. I cannot begin to imagine the chaos that Samuel Ingle's parents lived amongst with their large clan.

Thomas Ingle had four children with his first wife, Eliza Bacon. Eliza died in her early 30s, at which point Thomas married Harriet Jennings, twenty years his junior, who already had a baby girl when they met. The two of them went on to have another nine children, making a total of fourteen children between the two families.

The Ingle children were by no means little angels, and the local paper quite often had one of their names printed for various troubles or scrapes into which they got themselves, but none of the family appeared as frequently as Samuel Ingle.

At eight years of age, Samuel Ingle decided he did not want to attend the village school, and so he didn't! Schools for the poor were still a new concept at this time, and the poor did not attend school when Samuel was born. Schools were for the rich and not for the likes of the Ingles. However, the new Sandon Act that had been introduced earlier that year meant that the School Board now enforced school attendance up to the age of ten years. Samuel's non-attendance resulted in his parents' court appearance in Mildenhall's Court of Petty Sessions held in August 1876, where they were charged with not sending their child to school. Harriet Ingle spoke to defend herself:

"We have done all we can to keep Samuel at school, me and my husband wish he would do what is right".

The case was dismissed, and Harriet Ingle promised to keep the boy to his duty, so the Ingles were free to go without punishment.

They kept to their word and ensured Samuel was now attending the village school, not that he wanted to be there any more than he had previously, and I'm sure his teachers wished he wasn't there too! In November 1876, Samuel Ingle attacked Mr. Thresher, the master of the School Board at West Row. Thomas Ingle had walked his child to school and left him outside. Mr. Thresher went to bring him into the school when he was met with "very bad language". Samuel Ingle then kicked him violently on the knee. Once in the school room, the attack continued, and Samuel inflicted a "severe" wound on Mr. Thresher's knee.

Samuel Ingle was told he must leave the school. After being suspended from the school, Samuel decided to amuse himself each day by throwing stones at other children as they entered and left the playground and by shouting out to the teachers.

The Ingles found themselves in court again! Mr. Thresher said he would not have normally considered bringing this case to court, but the School Board had forbidden corporal punishment in the school, the result of which was this case of insubordination. Rev. E. Sparke, who was hearing the case, said, "The prohibition by the board was a mistake, and a good birching would have been beneficial to the boy". The bench decided they would sentence Samuel Ingle to two days imprisonment (at eight years old!) and a birching, if the father agreed to it. Not surprisingly, Thomas Ingle said he did not want his boy to have a flogging. As an alternative, the Ingles had a choice of being fined 10s 6d for the assault and 9s for expenses, or seven days imprisonment for the boy. Samuel's father after some time considering said, *"It would be beneficial for the boy to have the imprisonment"*, and Samuel was accordingly committed.

Rather than pay the fine, Thomas Ingle decided to send his eight-year-old child to be imprisoned. Samuel Ingle was locked up for the first time in his life, but it wouldn't be the last time either. It is unacceptable to us that any child of eight years of age could be locked up, irrespective of their behaviour. Many Victorians shared this sentiment, and reformers were asking questions as to how children who broke the law should be treated. They knew that locking them up with hardened criminals, as had previously been done, was not helping but at the same time, the Victorians believed in strict discipline. Children of Samuel's age had been routinely locked up at the beginning of the nineteenth century for the smallest of crimes, and thrown into jail with other prisoners regardless of age or crime. By the middle of the century, it was unusual for a child under the age of ten to be locked up, but the number of children imprisoned from ten years upwards rose steeply. The 1851 census of England shows that only twenty children under the age of ten were in prisons; however, between the ages of ten and fifteen there were eight hundred and seventy-five! So Samuel Ingle, imprisoned in 1876 at the age of eight, could consider himself treated extremely harshly. He would have been one of a few prisoners of his age in the country. It was not until 1908 that the imprisonment of children under fourteen was abolished.

Having served his relatively short period of time in jail, Samuel

Ingle was now back in West Row. Evidently his sentence did little to change his behaviour, and in December 1877, Samuel Ingle was again summoned to court. Samuel's crime this time was vandalising the new Board School, but he did not appear and the case was adjourned.

In 1878, Samuel Ingle's one-child vendetta against his village school continued. As the more compliant local children turned up to school, their hearts would have sunk, their bodies full of terror as they spotted their young contemporary, Samuel Ingle, stalking the playground with an iron wheel and a handful of stones. Samuel was now aged eleven and didn't even need to legally attend school, but nevertheless he continued his reign of terror against those who did attend.

In what now seems like a yearly event, Samuel Ingle appeared in the Mildenhall Court of Petty Sessions in November 1878, Mr. Thresher again giving evidence. *"On the day in question, I heard a noise outside, and on going there I saw the defendant trundling an iron wheel amongst the flowers in the garden in front of the school. Witness ordered him off upon which defendant called him foul names and threw stones at him. The boy had been very disorderly in school and was the terror of the other children."* Mr . Thresher's own children were also witness to the event, backing up their father's statements, and they also added that they saw Samuel Ingle knock the ornamental part of some railings off. The bench adjourned the case for further hearing in a fortnight, and in the meantime, ordered Samuel Ingle to attend the Board School himself. (I'm not sure Mr. Thresher would agree with that punishment).

The case was heard again a fortnight later, when Mr. Thresher stated that in the last fortnight, Samuel had behaved as well as any boy could behave, and his attendance was regular. The Court was pleased to hear this and discharged him. What an unexpected outcome! Either Samuel Ingle had massively changed his ways over the course of just two weeks, or Mr. Thresher had paid lip service to the court to draw a line under his time with Samuel Ingle. However, Mr. Thresher had more Ingle siblings to still go through his school, and in 1880, history had started to repeat itself when Samuel's father, Thomas Ingle was fined again for not sending children under the age of ten to school! Good luck, Mr. Thresher.

Samuel Ingle made it to his teenage years. He no longer terrorised the school children, that all being left behind him, so who would be next? In March 1883, at the age of fifteen, he was working as an agricultural labourer, when he was summoned to Court for being drunk and disorderly. He did not appear for his trial, and a warrant was issued for his apprehension. He did eventually attend the hearing in May 1883, when described as a promising youth, he was charged with being drunk and disorderly. On the seventeenth of March, P.C. Nunn had seen Samuel Ingle laying in the road in West Row, and he ordered him to get up. Ingle then began to use bad language and only stopped when P.C. Nunn was preparing to take him into custody. Harriet Ingle spoke at the case just as she had done seven years previously, defending her son. "Beer had been given to my boy".

The Chairman, not wanting to hear her story, responded, "It would have been better for the defendant to have obeyed the summons; by not doing so the expenses increased." It was stated that "six or seven years ago, Samuel Ingle had twice been convicted for assaulting his schoolmaster, Mr. Thresher, late of West Row", (poor Mr. Thresher had now died), "and has since been the annoyance of several people in West Row". Samuel Ingle was fined 14s or 14 days locked up in default of payment.

Following his latest court appearance, Samuel Ingle joined the Army, joining the Suffolk Regiment in 1884. At the age of sixteen, Samuel had lied on his application form, claiming to be eighteen years of age. Upon discovering his army record, I smiled to myself and felt hope for Samuel. Maybe this was what he needed, maybe he would respond to the strict discipline of the army. Hoping that Samuel could turn his life around, I was crossing my fingers for a promising army career. What we do learn from Samuel's army papers is that he was 5'6" tall (an average height for this era) and weighed 133lbs (9.5 stone).

Samuel's army career would see him serving in the East Indies, and as I read through his army records, the hope that I had for his reform melted away. In 1886, he was awaiting trial for using violence against his superior. There are echoes of his school life and the attack on Mr Thresher, and imprisonment and hard labour from his young civilian days had taught him nothing. Samuel was barely an adult, still a teenager, but very much in the tough adult world of the Army. Having attacked his officer, Samuel was either as hard as nails or had the intelligence of one!

Following his trial for the attack on a superior, Samuel was imprisoned between November 1886 and March 1887. On being released, he continued his service in the East Indies until 22nd March, 1892. Samuel's East Indies campaigns included the Hazara (Pakistan) expedition, also known as the Black Mountain Expedition. The British Army were fighting alongside the Gurkhas and Indians against local tribesmen in the mountains. On the Facebook page that accompanies this book, there is a photo of soldiers from Samuel's regiment, the 1st Suffolks during this expedition. Could he be in the photo? In 1888, Samuel was awarded the India War Medal with clasps for the Hazara expedition.

After leaving the army, Samuel Ingle moved back to West Row, the small village on the edge of the fens, a vastly different place to the East Indies where he had been stationed. It wasn't long before he found himself in trouble again.

I'm not quite sure anything summed up the Victorian era quite like a travelling menagerie, a touring group of showmen and animal handlers who visited towns and cities across the country with their exotic animals. At the end of the nineteenth century, there were several of these traveling menageries, but the largest and most popular was Wombwell & Bostock's. This menagerie had eighteen huge carriages and over six hundred animals available to them for their tours, including elephants, camels, rhinos, kangaroos, and obviously, big cats!

The Victorians had more social time available than previous eras, but did not travel far from their homes as entertainment would travel to them. The British Empire was strong and education had been reformed, the Victorians were hungry to learn (perhaps not Samuel Ingle) about science and the world around them. Charles Darwin's Theory of Evolution had caused controversy and challenged Christian ideas, but it also brought an interest in nature to the public. All these ingredients collided to make menageries immensely popular. Animals from all over the empire were collected, and the public not only wanted to learn about these animals, but they also had an interest in the menagerie staff members who were natives from countries around the empire. Most importantly, they wanted to be entertained.

The Victorians believed it showed great power and wealth to move these animals to Britain, keep them alive and tame them. There was a need to show power over nature, and lion tamers would amaze audiences by placing their heads in the mouths of lions and tigers. The public too could interact with these animals, and one menagerie had a jaguar reportedly so tame that the public queued up to let it lick their hands. Wombwell himself had a famous lion named Nero that allowed members of the public to enter its cage, (although this lion did later kill his handler).

The travelling animal shows had minimal thought for health and safety and very little consideration to animal welfare. Animals were travelling up and down the country to perform in these shows, staying for just one night before moving on in their carriages. If we assume they were not mistreated in their training, (I'm sure the training was probably not pleasant), travelling in cages along bumpy roads was not a great life for the animals.

Wombwell would also wager five thousands sovereigns that his lion could beat any six pit bull dogs in a fight. Thousands of people flocked to watch as the famous lion named Wallace tore the dogs to shreds, roaring in victory with blood pouring from its mouth. There is a very detailed report of this fight that took place in 1825. It is a sad window into Victorian pastimes, and the only positive from this spectacle was that they agreed to never match bulldogs against lions again.

There were also many deaths over the years of both members of the public and staff. I've read two separate incidents of a staff member falling from the carriage and getting run over by the wheels as the menagerie travelled between towns. Another death occurred when a boy was picked up and killed by an elephant, and another when a lion tamer was killed in Bristol in front of the audience, blood spraying from his neck as the lion named Nero tossed him around.

Although attacks happened, they were rare considering the number of shows that were put on, and in most cases, the show would arrive in town and entertain the public without any issues. Who would know what triggers an animal on a certain day to suddenly attack?

Wombwell's Menagerie, (later called Bostock & Wombwell's Menagerie), had visited Mildenhall regularly for many years, always well-advertised in the local press before the event. The menagerie would turn up with sixteen carriages, forty draught horses and a brass band. An advertisement in the Bury Free Press advertised that Bostock & Wombwells Menagerie would attend Mildenhall on

November 7th, 1881. The list of animals that would arrive was absolutely astounding! Listed below are just some of the animals I've picked out as highlights that were travelling to Mildenhall that year, as they set up their travelling show in the marketplace:

Antelope, pumas, wild boars, horned horse, brindled gnu, blue and red faced gorillas, yaxtruss, baboon, black dromedary, zebu, Brahmin cow, tapir, elephant, lions, tigers, leopards, bears, wolves and hyenas.

I'd feel fortunate to see that list of animals if I travelled to a zoo, let alone the local marketplace. I find it unbelievable that such an array of animals turned up at Mildenhall and other local towns in Suffolk each year, and I cannot find one photograph that documents this event in the town. There are, however, plenty of newspaper reports. I also find it hard to imagine how they squeezed all the carriages, horses, show animals and band into the marketplace. Oh, I wish I could find a photo! In Bury St Edmunds, they hosted the show on Angel Hill and in Newmarket on Severals, which are much larger areas of land.

On 10th April, 1894, the world famous Wombwell & Bostock's Menagerie was again visiting Mildenhall. What an event this must have been for the locals. It would be an extremely popular show if it attended the town today, in an age when we can instantly view images of any animals just by typing their name into a device in our pocket. For the Victorians to see these rare creatures and the animal keepers from all corners of the globe, must have seemed like real-life magical fantasy. I suppose the equivalent today would be a travelling show turning up with a carriage full of unicorns.

The Wombwell & Bostock lions visiting that day in April 1894 were well trained; Samuel Ingle was not. There would be no lion attack in Mildenhall, but an attack by Samuel Ingle was almost guaranteed. They had the wrong beast behind bars!

Samuel attended the event, as I'm sure a lot of locals would have done. He had drawn out his army reserve pay and had been "drinking freely and caused a disturbance". He was charged with "being drunk and riotous in Mildenhall market place". Samuel attacked Henry Bradley, an innocent bystander who had come to the show, and on being apprehended, Samuel then struck P.C. Bloomfield. Samuel was sentenced to seven days hard labour for being drunk and another seven days for attacking Henry Bradley.

In 1906, Samuel rejoined the army enlisting with the Suffolk

Militia. I'm sure by this point in the chapter you are now quite aware of the pattern his life followed, and have probably guessed already that trouble followed Samuel again! In 1907, he was tried by Court Martial for "conduct to the prejudice" and sentenced to twenty-one days detention. He was discharged on 18th May, 1907.

In 1915, Samuel Ingle found himself in the Mildenhall Union Workhouse. I have not discovered when or why he entered the workhouse—was he a pauper or using the infirmary?

He happened to be in the workhouse at the same time as another former soldier, Arthur Watts from Worlington, which is another small village close to Mildenhall. Arthur Watts had also been in the Suffolk Regiment and, like Samuel Ingle, had also served in the East Indies. Arthur arrived in the East Indies in December 1892, nine months after Samuel had returned home, so the two men would not have served in the army together. Arthur had also fought in the Second Boer War from 1899 to 1902, for which he received the South African medal.

Arthur Watts was from a family of shoemakers living and working from their home in The Street, Worlington. Since leaving the Army, Arthur had moved back to Worlington and had found work at Worlington Golf club as a caddy. Worlington was still a relatively new course at the time, having been founded in 1893.

Cambridge University Golf Club started playing at the Worlington Golf Course in 1901; the university students would travel on the train from Cambridge to Mildenhall and drop their clubs out the carriage window as the train sped passed the Worlington course. The students would then walk the couple of miles back down the track from Mildenhall train station to Worlington, before climbing over the fence to enter the course near the fifth hole. In 1922, a halt was built in Worlington which must have saved the legs of the students and damage to the clubs, but also ended what was probably a fun tradition.

At just forty-two years of age Arthur had started to lose his eyesight, which must have made his work as a caddy very difficult. Sometime around 1912, he found himself in the workhouse. Unfortunately, for him, it was at the same time as Samuel Ingle.

On the morning of 17th February, 1912, a group of men including Arthur Watts were sitting around the workshop after breakfast. The men would quite often use this workshop as a sitting room. The fire was burning and the men chatting away, when Samuel Ingle appeared in the room. Samuel immediately complained that the fire was too smokey and being a man of short temper, this obviously was a far bigger issue to Samuel Ingle than it would have been to anyone else.

Samuel walked to the fire and picked up the iron poker. After stirring the fire with the poker, he then turned to the man closest to him, a man named William Wiseman and pushed his chest with the poker, (a weapon of choice in the workhouse it seems). Samuel Ingle then turned to Arthur Watts and said, *"You can take it up if you like"*.

Watts responded, *"I can use the poker as well as you can"*. Samuel swung the poker at Watts, missing him, and instead hitting a box. On the second swing, he struck Arthur across the back, and with the third swing, the iron poker forcefully struck the victim fully in his face. With blood running down his face, Arthur Watts leaned against a bench waiting for help to arrive.

Arthur Watts was taken to the infirmary to be cleaned up by the nurse. Dr Francis Barwell, the medical officer at the workhouse, attended Arthur at 10.45 that morning. Arthur had bruising to the back and elbows, another bruise on his left leg, a deep cut that extended right through his lip and a fracture of his upper jaw. A piece of bone carrying two teeth was now loose. Dr Barwell sewed the lip up and wired the teeth together. He visited Arthur Watts a few times that week and found his condition *"satisfactory and improving"*.

While the medical staff were working on Arthur Watts, Samuel Ingle was being arrested by P.C. Arthur Brown. On his way to the police station, Samuel Ingle told P.C. Brown: *"The place was full of smoke, and old man Wiseman did not like me interfering with the fire, I pushed the old man and he fell against the bench. Watts then put his spoke in. He thinks himself cock of the walk"*

Dr Barwell had visited Arthur Watts a further three times since he had attended to his wounds, and each time the patient had improved. However, when attending on Tuesday, the 23rd of February, Dr Barwell found Arthur Watts in bed ill with a high temperature. At the same time, the doctor noted that two other female inmates, who for some reason had been placed in the male ward, were both deceased, having died from scarlet fever. The nurse told Dr Barwell that Arthur Watts had also had a bright rash the day before, but the rash had since faded and could now only just be seen.

Dr Barwell came to the conclusion that Arthur Watts was suffering from a very severe attack of scarlet fever. Arthur Watts passed away on Wednesday, 24th of February, 1915, one week after he was viciously attacked.

An inquest into the death of Arthur Watts was held at the Workhouse by the Deputy Coroner, Charles Gross. Nineteen men were at the inquest, including Odden Read, Chairman of the Board of Guardians and Charles Jessup, the Workhouse Master. Dr Bygott (Medical Officer for West Suffolk) informed the Deputy Coroner that the deceased had scarlet fever, and for that reason none of the men entered the room. Instead, they viewed the body through an open doorway. During the inquest into the death, Dr Barwell was asked if the injuries caused by Samuel Ingle had caused or in any way accelerated the death. Dr Barwell responded "I see no evidence whatsoever that they have".

Dr. Bygott, who carried out the post mortem, gave details of his findings which confirmed that Arthur had scarlet fever. Dr. Bygott was asked by the Deputy Coroner, *"Are you of the opinion the cause of death is scarlet fever?"* Dr Bygott responded *"I am."*

The Deputy Coroner continued, *"You have heard this man's jaw was fractured and the bruises caused by another inmate, but in your opinion did those injuries in any way accelerate the death?"* Dr. Bygott, *"I don't think so, I may say that in making the examination I paid particular attention to that particular point."* In summing up, the Deputy Coroner remarked, *"The evidence was clear and he need not refer to it, it pointed clearly to death by natural causes. If the jury also thought so it was their duty to bring in a verdict to that effect."* Death by natural causes was the verdict of the jury.

Samuel Ingle appeared in court at Mildenhall Petty Sessions a few days later, charged with inflicting grievous bodily harm with a bar of iron to Arthur Watts. After two weeks in Cambridge Prison, Samuel Ingle appeared *"somewhat forlorn"* with a *"stubby beard"*. One of the magistrates protested about him being sent to court in such a condition. Samuel Ingle was bound over to appear at the next Quarter Sessions at Bury St Edmunds.

Arthur Watts' life had come to a violent end, and although not the cause of his death, the attack in my opinion was the catalyst for the events that would see Arthur Watts die from scarlet fever. The disease was feared during the lifetime of Arthur Watts. It was mentioned in several of the books of Charles Dickens, and was a disease to which Dickens himself lost two of his sons.

Thankfully, we no longer fear this disease. It is a rare occurrence in the modern world, and if someone was diagnosed with the disease today, a course of antibiotics will mean that the patient is well again after twenty-four hours into the ten-day course of pills. This was a luxury which was not available to Arthur Watts.

Samuel Ingle, having spent yet more time locked up in prison for his assault on Arthur Watts, was a free man again. In 1939, he was listed as being at the White Lodge in Newmarket. The White Lodge was the name given to the Newmarket Union Workhouse, when the Second World War started in 1939. The White lodge was repurposed to a hospital; primarily to receive war casualties. Samuel Ingle lived a long life, never married and never seemed far from trouble. Samuel's later years were spent living in Bury St Edmunds, where he died in 1949 at the age of eighty-two.

CHAPTER TWELVE

William Graham 1849 – 1916

In an era where the poor had it hard, the Grahams had it the hardest. An entire novel could be written solely on the lives of the Mildenhall Grahams. It would be full of heartache, gruesome crimes, complicated family relationships, destitute and desperate individuals. This chapter will take us on a journey through the life of William Graham, and his wife and children who were left to rot in the workhouse before rising to become war heroes!

William Graham was born in 1849, one of eight children born to Robert Graham and Mary Graham (nee Mortlock). His father, Robert, was a lime burner, possibly one of the worst occupations in history. In the Victorian era, lime powder was required for plaster and building materials. This was obtained by heating lime rock in a kiln with temperatures up to 1100°C. The work was hot, exhausting, and dangerous. Lime rock emits poisonous fumes as it burns, so it was not unheard of for lime burners to lose consciousness and collapse into their own burning kilns. When the lime was extracted from the kiln, it then had to be neutralised. This was done by plunging it into water, which set it spitting and frothing violently. Any lime that landed on the skin would burn straight through, leaving horrible scars. If it got into the eyes, you would be blinded for life. Appropriately enough, the Graham family lived in Kiln Street, which was later renamed to "Cemetery Road", and is the same street we now know as "Kingsway", renamed as part of the King Edward VII coronation celebrations in 1902. The lime kiln was situated just beside what we now know as the "old Cemetery", the cemetery itself having utilised the old chalk pit. The Lime kiln still existed in Mildenhall relatively recently, having been used as an air raid shelter in the Second World War.

In January 1863, there was an extraordinary case of "robbing the dead" that occurred in Mildenhall. It took place at what is now called the old cemetery. At this time it was very much the current cemetery, as burials had only begun there seven years earlier in 1856. On first discovering this crime, I was sure that one of the perpetrators would be the William Graham upon whom we focus in this chapter. However, after hours or even days trawling through old newspaper reports, and looking at all the William Grahams living in Mildenhall at the time, I discovered (with the help of a Graham family descendant now living in Australia) that it was in fact his namesake and first cousin, William Graham, who was ten years his senior. The unfortunate family to fall victim to the grave robbers were the Childerstones, a family who lived and worked on Holywell farm. The farmhouse still stands in Holywell Row today, and one of the large barns has now been converted into a stunning house. The farm owner, Jonathan Childerstone, and his wife, Frances, had lost their only son in 1859, when he was just twenty-three years of age. Mr. and Mrs. Childerstone felt this loss so much that they decided no one should ever have the property he left behind. They agreed the precious articles should be buried alongside whichever of them was first to die and be buried.

Jonathan Childerstone died on Christmas Eve 1862 and was buried the following January. Frances kept to the agreement and placed in his coffin a gold watch and chain, a silver watch and chain, a handkerchief pin, a scarf ring, forty gold sovereigns, and two tin boxes that had belonged to their son.

Charles Docking, the sexton and grave digger for St. Mary's, Mildenhall Church, knew about the goods buried with Mr Childerstone and more than likely had dug the grave himself. Docking became the mastermind behind the grotesque robbery, and set about finding some minions to help him commit his crime.

One Monday evening in June 1863, a young man named Charles Bird was feeling down on his luck and miserable at having little money to his name. Walking down St. Andrews street, he stopped at the Three Kings (a public house that has long since disappeared from Mildenhall), for half a pint. Charles Docking was also in this pub at the time and spoke to Charles Bird about the items in the grave. Docking bought more beer for Bird before asking him if he would be one of a party that he was putting together to rob the grave. Charles Bird, being very vulnerable at the time, due to both his financial and drunken state, agreed to take part in the grave robbing.

Docking, along with Bird, walked over to the cemetery. William Graham was planting trees in the cemetery and was asked if he would join them in their plan. William Graham, much more open to the idea of stealing from the dead, agreed to the plan without any need to ply him with drink first. The three men returned to the Three Kings, where they drank more beer. Sometime later that night, fuelled by the beer Docking had bought them, Charles Bird and William Graham, under the command of Docking, robbed the grave of Jonathan Childerstone.

The crime was discovered a month later, on the 28th of July, by Mr. King, the stone mason. Mr. King was about to lay two large flagstones over the vault when he discovered that the vault had been entered. The brickwork from the sides was pulled down and lay in the bottom of the tomb, and the coffin lid of Jonathan Childerstone had been wrenched off. The inner leaden coffin had been cut in two with a chisel and knife.

Items of small value, such as the tins and handkerchief, were recovered from the scene, but Charles Docking had taken the money and the watches to sell in London. By this stage, a sobered up and remorseful Charles Bird had begun to tell friends and family of his involvement and how Charles Docking had not shared the money with himself and William Graham.

Charles Bird was arrested and pleaded guilty to the crime. The judge gave him three months hard labour at the county goal. Charles Docking and William Graham ran away to London. It appears they hid in plain view—they appear in all census records and lived in London with their wives and children, under their real names. Although all information about their age and town of birth is correct, I cannot find any newspaper report or criminal document that suggests they ever received punishment for their crime.

There was a warrant for their arrest in August 1863, with some brilliant descriptions of the two men the police wanted to apprehend, Charles Docking's description particularly sounds like a Disney villain, or perhaps more appropriately, a Dickens character. Below is the actual description as it appeared in newspapers across the country.

*"**CHARLES DOCKING**, a native of Mildenhall about 40 years of age, about 5 feet 9 inches high, very stout, large fat face, very large reddish-brown whiskers meeting under the chin, a wart about the size of a horsebean (and which is always very red), on the cheek, very bushy dark brown hair, hazel eyes; generally wears a high crowned black hat, loose alpaca coat, and dark waistcoat and trousers."*

The last newspaper article I can find on the case is from November 1863, and it mentions that Graham and Docking have still not been found. It seems that it was easy to evade the law in Victorian England.

I did walk down to the old cemetery myself, to have a look at the crime scene. The old cemetery is a very peaceful oasis of green space in what has become a very busy town. The old cemetery in Mildenhall is the one place in the town you can walk and truly be by yourself. A former chalk pit, it sits lower than street level and no one can see you, which must have aided the three robbers. Nature has now reclaimed many of the burial plots with large trees engulfing many of the headstones, and I wonder if some of these large trees were planted by William Graham on the night of the robbery. The Childertsone grave itself is now covered in ivy, which has spread over the flagstones that had been laid by Mr King, climbing up to the top of the obelisk, and covering the entire monument in green leaves. One hundred and fifty eight years later, the Childerstone grave still looks very grand (despite the ivy). It is one of the largest and most elaborate plots in the cemetery, and the stone work and inscriptions are still very clear to read. The plot now contains Mr. and Mrs. Childerstone and their son, all reunited. Finally they are resting in undisturbed peace.

Forgetting his grave robbing cousin and returning to the William Graham featured in this chapter, our William Graham was also no stranger to the court house, his crime of choice being repeatedly "drunk and riotous". William Graham, like most twenty-year-olds, enjoyed a good drink, which unfortunately for him in Victorian times landed you in trouble. In 1869, William Graham was fined eight shillings and six pence for being drunk with his friend, Matthew Gee.

Undeterred by his fine, William continued to enjoy himself a little too much, resulting in twenty-eight days hard labour in Bury Goal in 1871. On the night that had led to his arrest, William had been drinking at the White Hart in Mildenhall High street, (a pub that only closed in recent years). The landlady, Mrs. Beard, momentarily left the bar area, and when she returned, she noticed a bottle of whisky was missing. On questioning William Graham about the missing bottle, he ran out of the White Hart and down the High street. He was apprehended and searched by the local policeman, P.C. Mansfield, who found the stolen whisky in his possession. William Graham admitted the offence and blamed the fact he was drunk. In court, it was said, "*the prisoner was a sad example of the effects of habitual intoxication, from a drunkard he had become a thief*".

Victorians had an interesting relationship with alcohol, and there have been many studies carried out by interviewing Victorians and Edwardians. Two pieces of research on this interesting subject are "The Pub and People", which focused on interviews carried out between 1938 and 1942, and also Thompson's study in 1970, where people born between 1872 and 1906 were interviewed on their parents' drinking habits.

From these studies, it's clear that beer was an important part of working life, with many people drinking every day in their own homes. It was normal to send the eldest children out to buy the "*supper beer*"—a jug of beer from the closest public house. Drinking was encouraged for what they believed to be health reasons, and many working-class people used beer as a relaxation tool and to escape from their hard life, so they were drinking each night. It was accepted that you could be drunk at home, but was frowned upon and punished when drunk in a public house or street.

On release from prison, William Graham entered into a relationship with Alice Mary Fuller. They were married in 1875 and moved to St. Pancras in London, where they were living in Churchill Road at the time of the 1881 census. Alice's sister, Minnie Fuller, was also living with them.

In 1882, William and Alice's first child, Alfred James, was born. They did not stay in London for long, and by 1884, when their second child, Robert William Graham, was born, they were living back in their home town of Mildenhall.

William found work at the West Stow sewage works. The sewage farm was created in 1887 to deal with sewage from Bury St Edmunds. It was when they dug the trench for sewage pipes that they first discovered remains of Anglo-Saxon life in West Stow. Following the closure of the sewage works, an archaeological dig was carried out in the area in the 1960s. As a result of this dig, a large Anglo-Saxon village was discovered, and this village was reconstructed on the site and remains a popular tourist attraction today. All that now remains of the sewage works is the pumping station.

Life was not easy for the young couple, particularly for Alice, as William spent his money on drink and provided very little for his family on which to live. William drank their money away, while Alice and the children suffered with little food or clothing.

In the early 1880s, a new charity had been formed, The National Society for the Prevention of Cruelty to Children (NSPCC). This charity had been alerted to the behaviour of William Graham and his neglect of his family, and it was this charity that offered a lifeline to Alice and her young boys.

In 1890, William Graham was brought up in custody, charged with willfully ill-treating, neglecting and exposing his two children in a manner likely to cause them suffering or injury. The prosecution was undertaken by the newly formed NSPCC. The court heard that William Graham was able to work and was earning 18 shillings a week. Superintendent S.G. Reeve was called to give evidence, and he stated that on Monday he had visited the family house but no one was at home; the doors were all off and the windows out. There was no food whatsoever in the house, and nothing in the way of furniture except an old bedstead, the only coverings to which were an old counterpane (bedspread) and sheet. After he left the house, he saw the prisoner's two children, who were very dirty and had no shoes on their feet. He also saw the prisoner's wife (Alice), who was receiving food for which the vicar had paid.

The superintendent had known William Graham for five years, during which time he had been turned out of three of four houses for not paying the rent, and he understood the current home had no doors or windows, as the landlord had removed them due to the rent having not been paid. The eldest boy, Alfred, had a very bad cough and an abscess on his face. For a bed, they had a canvas bag full of straw and only one sheet and counterpane. P.C. Nunn testified to having frequently seen William Graham drunk on Saturday nights. The prisoner had been in constant work for nine months and had been employed by West Stow sewerage works. Alice Graham herself was called upon to give evidence, which must have been a daunting experience, but as she faced her husband, she stood strong and told the court that William had given her eight shillings on the Saturday, six shillings of which had to be paid to Mr. Gee. William then took the remaining two shillings back, along with all the food in the house. The magistrates said that William Graham had acted in a most unnatural manner and committed him to two calendar months of hard labour, while Alice and the children were ordered to the workhouse.

William now found himself back in the county gaol, while Alice and the children found themselves living in the workhouse, which at this time was the old workhouse located in the corner of St Mary's churchyard. Although it was an absolute last resort to enter the workhouse, and families would rather go without food and comforts than enter, the family would at least now be fed, have clean clothes and bedding, which was the exact help this young family needed. Without the intervention of the NSPCC, I'm not sure that Alice and her children would have survived.

Mr. and Mrs. Jessup were very good custodians of the workhouse and treated their inmates well. They had regular events for the children and families to brighten their days, although life in the workhouse had to be tough. This was written into law and audited by Poor Law Inspectors, but the Jessups still found ways to treat their inmates and lift the gloom of workhouse life. One such treat of which the young Graham boys would have been part was a picnic in 1893, which was reported in the local paper:

"WORKHOUSE PICNIC.—The inmates of the Mildenhall Workhouse, numbering about 60, had a most enjoyable outing on Thursday last, in the shape of a picnic on one of the heaths near the town. A capital tea was provided with the usual luxuries afterwards. The younger members indulged in cricket and other games, no effort was spared by Mr .and Mrs. Jessup (the master and matron) to make the outing a success, and the weather proved favorable. The inmates returned to the Workhouse about 9 o'clock."

Alfred and Robert, the young Graham boys, could not have

dreamt of a day like this before entering the workhouse. With food, shelter and friends, the Graham boys really were better off in the workhouse.

William Graham served his time for the neglect of his family, carrying out two months' hard labour. On release from prison, he also entered the workhouse, where he rejoined his wife and children. In the 1891 census, all four members of the family are listed as inmates of the workhouse. Alice's mental state was not good; a hard life had taken its toll, and she was listed as an imbecile on the 1891 census—imbecile being a professional term meaning she was "weak minded", terminology that has now fallen out of professional use.

William didn't stay in the workhouse long, and shortly after his arrival, he abandoned his wife and children to the workhouse, and like his namesake cousin, ran away to hide in London.

In 1901, eleven years after the Graham family had entered the workhouse, Alice was still an inmate, having been transferred to the new workhouse in Cemetery way (Kingsway) after its construction in 1895. Her mental state had now progressed to a stage where she was listed as a lunatic in the 1901 census.

Alfred Graham, the eldest child, left the workhouse and moved to Wisbech, a fenland town forty miles from Mildenhall. When living in Wisbech, Alfred lived at number 9 Sluice Row. Sluice Row was the most run-down part of this town, full of dilapidated cottages that were barely fit for inhabitation. Nevertheless, it was still a marked improvement on the accommodation he had had to endure as a child, as now at least he had doors and windows. The houses at Sluice Row were two up, two down workers' cottages built between 1740 and 1750; they had no facilities, meaning that a shared toilet was used by all the people living in this row. These houses did not get running water until the 1930s, but water could be obtained from a local pump. In the early 1900s, around the same time that Alfred lived in Sluice Row, the buildings in this street had been deemed unsuitable for accommodation. However, they continued to be inhabited until 1950, when they were finally designated as a slum and demolished.

Alfred joined the Army in 1901 and served in the Middlesex regiment. On his enlistment paperwork under the box titled "distinctive marks", it mentions a scar on his left jaw—could this be from the abscess on his face which was mentioned during the trial for his father's neglect? Alfred embarked for South Africa to fight in the second Boer War in February 1901, for which he won an African War medal and clasps.

Alfred's younger brother had also left Mildenhall and moved to the fens. Robert Graham, seventeen years old at the time of the 1901 census, was working at Palmer's Farm in Burnt Fen and was also living with the Palmer family. His occupation is listed as a *"Horse Carter on farm"*.

In 1903, Robert Graham, like his older brother, joined the army. Robert served with the Royal Engineers, where he had a very good army career, taking advantage of the training and development offered to him. Robert became a qualified submarine mining swimmer, and a skilled blacksmith, which was later improved upon when he became a blacksmith superior.

His military career took him to Singapore, Australia, and of course, to France in the First World War.

On the 30th of August 1905, while Robert was serving in Singapore, he witnessed an attempted suicide. A local woman, shortly after midnight, had thrown herself into the rough sea. There was a strong current at the time and a risk of sharks, but Robert Graham dived into the sea to save her life. For his heroic act, he was awarded a bronze Humane Society award. Formed in 1774, this society gives out yearly awards for those that have risked their own lives to save that of another person or persons. Growing up in the workhouse, Robert had witnessed at first hand desperately broken souls who felt there was no way they could live in the world that constantly beat them down. Robert and his brother had survived a tough childhood, with little food or shelter, rags for clothes, and abandoned by their father, and with a mother too ill to leave the workhouse. Despite this constant drubbing by life, they had survived! Robert knew that the cycle of sadness in life can be broken. Robert's life had been saved by the NSPCC, who identified and removed the young boys from the neglect of their father, and the Mildenhall Board of Guardians and the Jessups, who provided them the relief they needed in the workhouse. Robert owed them his life and had now repaid society.

While Alfred and Robert were in the army posted overseas, serving their country and generally being good guys in this world, their poor mother, Alice, remained in the Mildenhall Union

Workhouse. She now listed herself as a widow, it being not uncommon to claim the status of a widow to escape the stigma of being abandoned. In reality, Alice was not a widow at all but a victim of bigamy. Too poor to divorce, her husband William Graham had remarried anyway and was now living in Anatola road, Islington, with his new wife, Mary Jane Graham, and working as a bricklayers' labourer.

William might have run away and escaped his life in Mildenhall, but he could not escape the workhouse, and from 1901 forward, there are regular entries for William Graham in the admission books of various workhouses around the St Pancras area. Sometimes he is listed as having no address, whilst another time he is recorded as being married to Mary Jane, and her address is listed. Her address changes over the years, but it is always around the Islington area. Of course, the William Graham who is seen regularly in the London Workhouse admission books could have been another William Graham of the same age, however, in the 1911 census we find the undeniable evidence that it is, in fact, the same William Graham who abandoned his family in Mildenhall.

The 1911 census lists a William Graham born in **Mildenhall in 1849**, (this is our Graham), as an inmate of St Anne's Home, St Pancras Auxiliary Workhouse. This is not only confirmation that William Graham could not escape the poverty to which he had abandoned his family, but also confirmation that he was alive and guilty of bigamy. Was William still spending all his money on his drinking habit? The changing of addresses and the fact he is sometimes listed as homeless suggests he was still being evicted from houses and failing to keep up rental payments.

The St Anne's Home Workhouse in which we find William Graham in the 1911 census had originally been the Royal Asylum of St Anne's Society, erected in 1829 to provide education for poor children. It was a grand regency period building, three stories high, finished with a cornice and parapet wall. The front of the building had a large four-column portico.

It was a fantastic piece of architecture that now only exists in images from the time, the building having been torn down in 1938 to build a block of flats now named Pullman Court. Without doubt, if the building had survived a few decades longer, it would now be afforded protection as a listed building. Ironically, the block of flats built in its place in 1938 is now a grade II listed building in its own right, due to the Art Deco design of the flats.

At the time of the 1911 census, Alfred and Robert were still both serving in the British Army—Alfred with the 1st Battalion Middlesex Regiment out in Singapore, while Robert was in Queensland, Australia, both having now escaped the shadow of the workhouse; a feat their parents had not yet managed. In the 1911 census, both parents can be found as inmates of workhouses, and it is no surprise that Alice Graham still remained an inmate at Mildenhall. She had now been an inmate of the Mildenhall Union for over twenty-one years! There really seems to have been no way out for Alice, who was just as poor as the day she entered. The 1835 Poor Law Act punished the poor for being poor, for needing help and being a burden on the rate payers. Alice was an example of the poverty trap created by this Act.

As elated as she must have been to see her sons walk away and emerge from the shadow cast over them by the towering oppressive walls of the workhouse, walking through the gate and on to the freedom to live their own lives, she now found herself just as lonely as she was poor. Sadly, for Alice, the reality for someone like her was that there was no way out. When Alice entered the workhouse, she must have known it could be a life sentence for her. It was the best option she had available to give her boys any chance in this world, and she needed the relief offered by the system.

The care of children in workhouses was extremely questionable, and there were many reports up and down the country of the abuse suffered by children at the hands of workhouse staff. The children being removed from their parents on arrival and with minimal contact with their parents, it was all too easy for evil staff members to target children. The biggest scandal came to light in 1894 at Brentwood, where children were being beaten with stinging nettles, forced to drink toilet water, kneel on wire netting and woken in the middle of the night and forced to parade around with baskets of clothes on their head. If any item fell out of the basket, they were beaten. Large scandals would make the papers if they were discovered, such as the case at Brentwood. Sadly, as with any abuse, I think a lot of incidents went unreported and unpunished, through fear or shame.

However, I have never found any articles detailing issues associated with the care given by the Mildenhall staff. In Odden Fredric Read, they had a true gentleman as their Chairman, a local man who loved the town and who had done everything he could to see the Mildenhall Workhouse and its people thrive. He was a man who had done his best to help the children who were in the care of the guardians leave the workhouse, and where necessary the Board of Guardians found the children foster care and work (if they were old enough). The Jessups ran the Mildenhall Union Workhouse, and there were never reports of poor cleanliness or mistreated inmates. I don't pretend the Mildenhall Workhouse was a jolly happy place to be— far from it as the work was tough, the food was basic, families split and inmates segregated, but this was all written into law, and the Jessups couldn't change this. I do believe the Board of Guardians and the Jessups did their best by their inmates, despite the rules dictated to them from the government following a now outdated Act.

The First World War was only a few years away; and Robert and Alfred would both see action on the front line and after escaping the harsh life of the workhouse, they would have to go through the horror of life in the trenches. Robert did not serve throughout the entire war, as in February 1916, he reached the period of engagement required when he enlisted, and as he was an existing soldier when the war broke out, he was entitled to be discharged. He took the opportunity to do this and with the life he had already had, no one could blame him. This was not the freedom for which he was looking. Robert was removed from the front line and returned home. He was awarded the Star Medal for his time spent serving his country in the war.

The admittance records for their father, William Graham, at various London Workhouses, cease in 1916. The last record sees William enter St Pancras Workhouse, this being William's last admission, as his life had come to a fitting end. Having spent a large majority of his existence in workhouses and after abandoning his wife and children to Mildenhall Workhouse, William Graham died as an inmate at St Pancras. On the 14th of June, 1916, aged 68 years, William passed away with the cause of death being certified as (1) Myocardial Degeneration and (2) Bronchitis. The certificate showed St Pancras Workhouse as his place of death and his address as 33 Islington Street.

The informant was the workhouse matron.

Alice Graham, now an actual widow, continued her life in the confinement of the workhouse. However, she had to be transferred to Newmarket. During the war, Mildenhall Workhouse, like many other workhouses across the country, was taken over by the army for military use. All the inmates of the Mildenhall Union Workhouse were transferred to Newmarket Workhouse (White Lodge).

Newmarket Workhouse was located on the North Side of Exning Road, and the building remains today. Like so many of the workhouses up and down the country, the Newmarket Workhouse transitioned into a hospital as workhouses were finally phased out after the Second World War. When a new hospital was built in Newmarket, the old workhouse was repurposed as residential flats, and is now a Grade II listed building.

Ten years prior to Alice Graham's relocation to Newmarket, King Edward VII had visited the Newmarket Workhouse. This was a very rare occurrence indeed, and during his visit, he met a young man named John Watts, an orphan who had worked locally as a stable lad.

John Watts was suffering from consumption and was in a confused state, and upon noticing a mandolin close to the bed the King asked John Watts if he played it. The Workhouse Master answered for him saying that the young man would like to play "God Save the King". The King set the stable lad at ease with a smile and encouraged him to do his best, and then the King further delighted John Watts when he told him how well he had played.

The poor of society dreaded entering the workhouse, a prison for those who had not committed a crime. It really was a last resort for a desperate person or family.

In 1846, an inmate of the Newmarket Workhouse named James Withers Reynolds, a resident of the nearby village of Fordham, superbly expressed these feelings in a poignant poem written to his sister. James and his family were inmates at Newmarket, but his sister was living in Cambridge. James wrote the poem from inside the workhouse walls, and although life was hard, his words show he could smile through it:

Since I cannot, dear sister, with you hold Communion.
I'll give you a sketch of our life in the Union.
But how to begin, I don't know, I declare;

Let me see: well, the first is our grand bill of fare.
We've skilly for breakfast, at night bread and cheese,
And we eat it and then go to bed if we please.
Two days in the week we've pudding for dinner,
And two we have broth, so like water, but thinner,
Two, meat and potatoes, of this none to spare;
One day bread and cheese and this is our fare.
And now then, my clothes I will try to portray;
They're made of coarse cloth and the colour is grey.
My jacket and waistcoat don't fit me at all,
My shirt is too short or else I am too tall;
My shoes are not pairs, though of course I have two,
They are down at the heel and my stockings are blue.
But what shall I say of the things they call breeches?
Why mine are so large they'd have fitted John Fitches.
John Fitches, you say, well pray who was he?
Why one of the fattest men I ever did see.
Neither breeches, nor trousers, but something between
And though they're so large, you'll remember I beg,
That they're low on the waist and high on the leg.
And no braces allowed me, oh dear, oh dear!
We are each other's glass so I know I look queer.
A sort of Scotch bonnet we wear on our heads,
And I sleep in a room where there are just fourteen beds.
Some are sleeping, some are snoring, some talking, some playing,
Some fighting, some swearing, but very few praying.
Here are nine at a time who work on the mill,
We take it by turns so it never stands still
A half hour each gang, so 'tis not very hard,
And when we are off we can walk in the yard.
We have nurseries here, where the children are crying,
And hospitals too for the sick and the dying.
But I must not forget to record in my verse,
All who die here are honoured to ride in a hearse.
I sometimes look up at a bit of blue sky
High over my head, with a tear in my eye,
Surrounded by walls that are too high to climb,
Confined as a felon without any crime.

Not a field, nor a house, nor a hedge I can see
Not a plant, nor a flower, not a bush, nor a tree,
Except a geranium or two appear
At the Governor's window, to smile, even here.
But I find I am got too pathetic by half,
And my object was only to cause you to laugh.
So my love to yourself, your husband and daughter,
I'll drink to your health in a tin of cold water,
Of course we've no wine nor porter nor beer,
So you see that we all are teetotallers here.

Alfred joined his brother in returning to Britain after a victorious but costly war for the country. The Mildenhall Workhouse never reopened, which was a constant source of debate locally. Alice Graham remained at the Newmarket workhouse, where she passed away, aged seventy-nine in 1930, her cause of death being recorded as degeneration of heart muscle and senile decay. Alice had spent forty years, more than half her life, in a workhouse.

CHAPTER THIRTEEN

Eliza Graham 1860 –1890

Eliza Graham is the sister of William Graham from the previous chapter, and although I did not wish to focus too much on one family, this family have enough interesting happenings to warrant the focus. It would have been possible to write an entire book on this family! It was too hard to choose just one member to write about, so this chapter will tell the life of Eliza Graham, another poor inmate of the Mildenhall Union, another poor member of the Graham family.

The Graham family did not always make up the numbers in the Victorian slums. In Georgian England, they were once a family of great wealth. To understand the destitute situation the Graham family find themselves in during Eliza's lifetime, it's worth looking back at Eliza's great-grandfather, a man who had it all and lost it all.

The Graham family first put down roots in Mildenhall in 1762, when Eliza Graham's great-grandfather, James Graham, married Frances Snare. A Mildenhall resident, he moved to the town from Stowmarket. The Graham family descended from a very wealthy branch of Grahams in Scotland. In 1792, a sum of £100 (around £15,000 would be an equivalent value today) was left to a James Graham in Suffolk. This money was inherited from a Peter Graham, who was part of an old Baronial Scottish family. This ties the Suffolk Grahams to the wealthy Scottish family.

When James Graham moved to Mildenhall in 1762, he was a wealthy man with a successful wig making business. In 1781, after being left a vast amount of money by his uncle Patrick Graham (another descendant of the wealthy Graham clan), James Graham bought the Crown pub and surrounding fields in Stoke by Nayland.

Mildenhall once had its own Bridewell in the town. It had just two rooms, the lower eleven feet by ten, and the upper twelve feet by eight. It had neither fireplace nor sewer. By 1790, the small Bridewell was no longer required after the Bury St Edmunds Goal had been built. This very same Bridewell in Mildenhall was bought by Eliza's grandfather, Johnathon Graham (son of James), and on the documentation he is also listed as a peruke maker (long curly men's wigs). The Bridewell in Mildenhall stood in what is now Queens' Way, but was previously known as West Street, and before that Bridewell Street. The old Bridewell was demolished sometime before 1812, and the site stood empty for a few years before a cottage was built in its place in 1834. In 1870, a second house was also built on the old Bridewell land, and these two houses still survive today as numbers 81 and 83 Queensway.

In 1803, a decade after acquiring the old Bridewell, James Graham was declared bankrupt. This coincided with the men of that period wearing their hair in a more natural state. The boom of men's wig making had come to an end, and men had stopped the use of the periwigs and perukes associated with fashion in the Georgian era (a fashion which, fingers crossed, will never be revisited.) This obviously would have had a huge impact on James Graham's peruke business.

Bankruptcy in Victorian times was a crime and was punished with a very public shaming. It was a process designed to humiliate the individuals and families concerned, and details of a person's bankruptcy were printed in the London Gazette, and then picked up by the local newspapers. This embarrassment was handed out to James Graham, who had his bankruptcy reported in the London paper as well as the local press. On top of the public shame of bankruptcy, it also came with a prison sentence (up until 1869). As part of James Graham's bankruptcy his property in Mildenhall Market Place was sold, at which time its particulars were listed as consisting of a large parlour, hall and shop, five good bed chambers, two garret rooms, kitchen, backhouse and offices, with a yard and gardens. I do not know which building this would have been in the marketplace, as the buildings in the marketplace predate James

Graham. My assumption is that his property may still be standing today, although I'm unsure which house would have belonged to the Grahams.

We now pick up the timeline of the Grahams again in the mid 1800s, now one of the poorest families to reside in Mildenhall, this being a real-life riches to rags in the space of fifty years. Many of the family members at some point lived in the workhouse for a period of time, some for decades or even the majority of their lives.

Eliza Graham was born in 1860, one of eight children of Robert and Mary Graham, including William Graham from our previous chapter. In 1877, a young Eliza fell pregnant at the age of seventeen, at which point she married a local man named Walter Henry Ranns from Kennett, a small village just five miles from Mildenhall. The couple were wed in St. Mary's Mildenhall Church.

There is a strong connection between the Graham family and London, particularly the St. Pancras area. Many of the family members married in Mildenhall and moved to St Pancras. Eliza also followed this path. After their wedding, a pregnant Eliza and her husband moved to Charlton Road, Somers Town, St. Pancras. Somers Town was certainly one of the more affordable neighbourhoods in London, as it had been populated by the poorer citizens of France at the end of the previous century. As the French fled the horrors of the French revolution, when arriving in London they were attracted to Somers Town by the cheap rents in this area.

Eliza and Walter settled in St. Pancras where Walter worked as a horse keeper. Four months after their arrival in the capital, their baby girl was born, whom they named Emily.

Two years later a second child was born, this time a son named Charles Henry. All was well in the world of Eliza at this time, but obviously being part of the Graham family, and indeed part of this book, you can hazard a guess it wouldn't remain this way.

In 1881, Eliza's husband, Walter Ranns, passed away, yet again a young Victorian man cut down in his prime by the dreaded disease consumption. This left Eliza with no income and two young children for whom to care. In the Victorian era, if you lost your husband, which was a far too common occurrence, you needed to remarry fairly rapidly to be able to feed and care for both yourself and your family. Eliza moved her family back to Mildenhall, and in 1882, married her second husband, Arthur William Morley, a blacksmith who lived in Mildenhall on Beck Row Road. At this time, the road to Beck Row would have continued from Folly Road across what is now the airbase, before joining up with the street in Beck Row, the main road we now use to travel to Beck Row. This road goes around the Base perimeter, which did not exist until after the Base was built in the 1930s.

Eliza and her new husband, Arthur, had a further three children, Rosa, born 1883, Sarah Ann, born 1885 and Arthur William, born in 1887. The eldest child, Rosa, was classified as an "Imbecile from birth". This word is no longer used as a medical term, and it is now only really used as an insult, but in Victorian England it was used to describe a person who was unable to look after their own affairs due to being "weak minded". The Victorians had a poor understanding of mental health conditions, and grouped people together as either imbeciles or lunatics so there is no way of knowing Rosa's exact disability.

Eliza's second marriage did not create a loving environment for her or her five children, as after the death of her first husband, she married for security rather than love and ended up with neither. In 1889, Eliza, Arthur and their family were struggling and had spent some time living with Arthur's mother, Sophia Morley, in West street (now Queensway). The house was situated towards the end of the street going out of Mildenhall towards West Row; it was conveniently situated close to both the Queen's Arms and another former public house The Gardeners Arms, which closed its doors in the early 1900s, but would have been fully functional at this time to service Arthur's needs.

On a bitterly cold winter evening on 9th of November 1889, Eliza and her children were walking through Mildenhall Town, desperately trying to find food or shelter. The family were living a nomadic lifestyle at this point, sheltering wherever and with whomever they could each night. The family sometimes stayed at her sister's house, that of Elizabeth (Lizzie) Graham. Although Lizzy Graham would try and help, she could not offer much in the way of shelter and comfort having very little herself. When staying with Eliza's sister, the family would sleep on bricks.

Her husband, Arthur Morley, had given Eliza sixpence the

previous day, which she had spent on bread that had been consumed by her hungry children. Eliza and her children had no food during the day of 9th November and so went to the local vicar who gave her another loaf of bread. The cold and hungry family walked to Fullers' Yard where Eliza's mother lived.

Fullers' Yard is an area of Mildenhall that no longer exists; it was situated somewhere off what is now Kingsway. On the census records, they are listed just after the cottage hospital (which is next to the old cemetery). I have been told there was a lane that led to the nine old and rather small cottages, probably on the Maid's Head side of the road. The nine dilapidated cottages were just about fit for human habitation. In 1913, these buildings were condemned under the "Housing and Town Planning Act" before being demolished. I have asked several older residents of Mildenhall where Fullers' Yard was located and no one I've spoken to seems to know the exact location.

When Eliza and her children reached Fullers 'Yard, the children, dressed in rags, were crying with hunger. The cottages were small and, like her sister, Eliza's mother could not offer her much in the way of shelter or food. It was a freezing cold November night, and Eliza and her children were able to shelter in the shed of a neighbouring cottage, belonging to the sheep shearer Alfred Petley. The shed housed a long wagon and had no front door, offering only minimal shelter from the winter.

In the morning the children were shivering, cold and crying. Eliza warmed them by her mother's fire before walking to the police station where she reported her husband for neglect. The police officer arranged for them to go to the workhouse. Eliza had not previously entered the workhouse under instruction of her husband, who did not wish his family to stay there.

Charles Jessup, the workhouse master, met the family at the workhouse. Eliza was carrying a crying child in her arms who had no shoes on, and it was another bitterly cold morning. In a court hearing, Charles Jessup had the following recollection of that morning: *"The child's feet were blue with cold, this was the imbecile child. The other three children were standing by the mother crying, they were scantily clad and their feet were through the shoes"*. Charles Jessup took them into the workhouse and supplied them with food which they eagerly ate.

"Three months after entering the workhouse the imbecile child who was

about eight years old could now nearly run on her own, when on entering could not even stand by herself."

Arthur Morley was charged with neglect of his children in what was the first prosecution in Mildenhall under the new Act for preventing cruelty to children. The magistrates, after considering the evidence, sentenced Arthur Morley to one month's imprisonment with hard labour.

What was not mentioned in the court case or reported in the newspaper write up, was that Eliza was five months pregnant on that freezing cold night and seven months pregnant when the case went to trial. I would have thought this would have been a key detail and evidence in a neglect case, which makes me wonder if Eliza even knew she was pregnant herself. It makes the lack of food and care for herself and family even more heartbreaking. The other detail omitted in the case is that Eliza's eldest child, ten-year-old Charles Ranns, was not with his mother during this entire ordeal, and never entered the workhouse with his mother.

Eliza and her four youngest children were now sheltered, clothed and fed. They were much better off in the workhouse and should have entered a lot sooner. The poorest members of the parish, who needed aid from the Mildenhall poor Union, often would not enter the workhouse due to the stigma attached with doing so. It definitely caused Arthur Morley more embarrassment to allow his family to tramp the streets of Mildenhall, crying dressed in rags, than it would have done to enter them into the workhouse.

As I write this, my youngest boy has just come to sit on my lap, perfect timing to give him an extended hug and reflect on how lucky my wife and I are to have a loving family environment for our children to grow up, where they will never be short of food, heating and the odd luxury. Poor Eliza at times could not even offer her crying child a crumb of bread or suitable winter clothing as they walked the streets.

In March 1890, Eliza was to give birth to her sixth child, and this would turn out to be the final tragic event in Eliza's short life. Eliza's newborn, who she had named Alfred, died shortly after his birth. On the 17th March, Eliza also passed away, aged twenty-nine, only 14 days after she had given birth to baby Alfred. The main cause of death is listed as *"childbirth 14 days"* but a second cause is *"Pneumonia 9 days"*.

Childbirth was still a very dangerous event at this time and continued to be so until the mid-20th century. In 1900, the annual death rate per one thousand births for maternal mortality was forty. Eliza was now part of this grim statistic, as after the birth of her child she had developed pneumonia leading to her eventual death.

Eliza's five surviving children were now effectively left orphaned, as Arthur Morley never took any of them back in to live with him. In 1894, Arthur Morley remarried. His new wife, Hannah Perfect, was from Blything. After they married, they lived in Westhall on the East Suffolk coast. Arthur and Hannah did not have any children together. On the 1911 census, under "total children born alive" Arthur wrote "none".' In the 1891 census, Eliza's children Emily, Rosa, Sarah Ann and Arthur are shown as all still living at the workhouse. They had now been joined by their aunt, Alice Graham, and their cousins Robert and Alfred, who were also now in the workhouse following the child neglect trial of William Graham detailed in the previous chapter. On the census record, the child's aunt (Alice Graham) is listed directly after that of Rosa, Sarah and Emily but before the four year old Arthur William's name. Alice's name being inserted between that of her young nieces and nephew to me indicates that she was able to help look after these children whilst they were all in the workhouse together, listed as a family unit.

The young children had another familiar face to help care for them in the workhouse. Also, on the 1891 census another family member appears in the workhouse. It was Lizzie Graham, Eliza's sister, the same sister who used to offer Eliza and her children what little she could when they were desperate for food and shelter. Lizzie does not appear as an inmate but as a "servant" listed under the names of the Jessup family and before the names of the listed inmates. I like to think that Mr. and Mrs. Jessup offered this role to Lizzie to help look after the many Graham family members in the workhouse. After all, Lizzie had six nieces and nephews all living in the workhouse, as well as a brother (William Graham) and sister-in-law (Alice Graham).

Thanks to the census record of 1891, the whereabouts of Eliza Graham's eldest son Charles Ranns is revealed. He was living in Hollywell Road (which we now know as Field Road) with other members of the Graham household. In total, there were ten members of the family living here at this time in what is essentially a home for some of the waifs and strays of the Graham family. The relationships between the members of this household are quite complicated. It is interesting to look at the relationship between the household members, and to understand how this family helped each other out. They were a poor family that pulled together to survive.

The head of this household was sixty-two year old Charles Graham, the uncle of Eliza Graham (great uncle of Charles Ranns). He is a widower twice over having lost two wives at a young age, the first wife at twenty-three years old and his second wife at thirty-six years of age. The next family member listed in this household is that of Eliza's sixty-four year old mother (grandmother of Charles Ranns). We know that she was living in the dilapidated cottages in Fullers' Yard previously, now a year later she was living with the brother of her late husband. Charles Graham's daughter, Emma Mortlock (née Graham) and her five girls (Annie, Lilian, Ellen, Florence and Elizabeth) were also living here. Emma had become a widow the previous year when her husband Ambrose Mortlock had passed away. The youngest member of the household was the one year old William Robert Graham, the son of Lizzie Graham (who was living and working at the workhouse). The tenth and final member of this busy, and what must have been noisy, household was Eliza's twelve-year-old son, Charles Ranns. I am very pleased that at least one of Eliza's children had been kept out of the workhouse and was living in what very much appears to have been a caring household.

The youngest member of the "waifs and strays" household, William Robert Graham, the cousin of Charles Ranns and nephew of Eliza Graham, is a name that once again led me to the Mildenhall War Memorial. It has really surprised and saddened me just how often during my research I have ended up looking up the name of another who had died in the First World War.

William Robert Graham was born to Lizzie Graham in 1890, and his father's name is not listed on the birth certificate. His mother, Lizzie, married John Albert Foreman in 1892, and over the next nine years they had five more children before another cruel and tragic twist of the Graham family. Lizzie died at thirty-two years of age in 1901, leaving the eleven year old William and his brothers and sisters without a mother. In the 1901 census, having lost his mother, William Robert was living with his stepfather, brothers and sisters and step-grandfather in Mildenhall Church yard, in one of the last houses before the High Street (next to what is now Martins Furnishers).

In 1911, the now twenty-two year old William Robert Graham was living with his stepfather John Foreman, who had now remarried. John Foreman's new wife was Annie Graham, the daughter of Emma Mortlock (née Graham) and one of the girls who was living with William Robert at the "Charles Graham Waifs and Strays" in 1891. This unconventional family was also now living at Fullers' Yard, the mysterious location of run-down old cottages. Fullers' Yard was condemned and torn down just two years after this census record.

William Robert Graham was killed in action in 1917 in Egypt. The Bury Free Press reported his death on the 19th May 1917:

ANOTHER MILDENHALL HERO:-

...Prvt. William Robert Graham, who, we regret to state, was killed in action, whilst serving with the Egyptian Expeditionary Force, on April 19th. He enlisted in the 7th Suffolk Regiment in February 1915, and went the following August to France, where he was wounded three times. He was home on sick leave in December last, and on draft leave in January, when he was transferred to the 5th Suffolk's, and went to Egypt to join them there. Only a few days before his death he wrote a very cheery letter home, saying he was having a good time out there with the Mildenhall boys, and there was not much fighting going on just then.

After going off on a very worthwhile tangent to remember another fallen young soldier listed on the Mildenhall War Memorial, let us get back to Eliza Graham's immediate family and look at what happened to her five surviving children; did they escape the shadow of the workhouse to have brighter futures?

Charles Ranns, the son who had managed to avoid the workhouse, found employment at the Mildenhall Gas Works. In 1901, at twenty-two years of age, Charles was living with the gasworks manager Mr. Davenport and his wife at "the Riverside Gas Works ", his occupation being listed as "Gas worker". In 1912, Augustine Davenport, the gas works manager, was found dead, drowned in the gas pool out the front of his house. This discovery shocked the town.

The gas works were established in 1838, opened in 1840, and built alongside the river Lark just over the bridge in Mill Street. The gas manager lived in the first house on the left as you cross the bridge. The area of water here is still known as "the gas pool".

The gas works provided gas for the street lamps and gas for

cooking stoves and fires. Every evening, the lamplighter would tour the streets of Mildenhall with his ladder and light the street lamps. Many people complained about the dimness and high charges of this service. In the early 1900s, the Parker Brothers (owners of the flour mill) offered to light the town with electricity, which prompted the gas works to expand. In 1902, shares were issued and a new gasometer (gas holder) was built; also at this time the roads were dug up to extend the gas service along Kingsway to the workhouse and out along North Terrace to the new school (St Mary's School). Electric lights were installed in 1936, and the gasworks closed in 1958. The structures at the gasworks were demolished in the 1970s.

In October 1901, Charles Ranns married Annie Saunders Foreman at St Mary's Mildenhall Church, and after their marriage they lived in Church walk where together they had three children; Florie (1903), Jessie (1904) and Charles (1906) who were all born in Church Walk.

In 1911, Charles Ranns was working as a "cowman on a farm", and the Ranns family were living in St Andrews Street, which is the street that leads from the town towards the Church. This street had once been named Chalk Lane but was later changed to Cock Inn Lane because the Inn of the same name sat opposite the road. What was the Cock Inn is today split into shops and cottages. A rather big sprawling inn, which was located in the buildings we know as 28-32 High Street (now Spice Lounge and Martins Furnishers). The Inn continued round the corner of the church yard and back onto Mill Street, as well as the yard area in between these buildings (which now houses a dog groomer). The Bell Hotel opened at the start of the nineteenth century and took much of the Cock Inn's trade, and the Cock Inn eventually closed in 1821. The street leading to it was renamed after the Church, which at that time was dedicated to St Andrew. In 1895, it was discovered that the Church of Mildenhall was originally dedicated to St Mary. The Church on this discovery reverted back to its original name but St Andrews Street never changed accordingly, and today we still call this road St Andrews Street.

The Ranns' household was situated at one end of St Andrews street, where Costa Coffee now stands. The long white house Charles Ranns and his family lived in was torn down in the 1980s, but can be seen over on our Facebook page, along with pictures illustrating each chapter in this book.

At the outbreak of the First World War, Charles Ranns travelled to Newmarket to enlist into the Suffolk Regiment. His enlistment date is 1st February 1915, which is a year before compulsory conscription began. On his enlistment paper his occupation is given as "milkman". The paper also allows us to formulate an image of Charles in our heads, as he was described as a short man even for the time period, standing at just 5 feet 3 inches tall and weighing 8.5 stone, which is actually the minimum height the army accepted, the restriction having been lowered from 5 feet 4 inches the previous November. Interestingly, the British Army did create "bantam battalions" following complaints from volunteers who were turned away for being too short. In total 29 Bantam Battalions were set up for men who stood between 5 feet and 5 feet 3 inches. Charles Ranns just scraped by into a regular battalion.

Charles embarked for France from Felixstowe on 11th August 1915. On 30th December of the same year, he was wounded in the field when he was shot in the face. He was admitted to hospital the same day where he stayed a week before returning to duty.

On the 24th August 1918, Charles was again injured, this time from shell gas. He was gassed while fighting on the front line in Armentieres, and following the gassing, he spent six weeks in hospital with general weakness. He returned to duty to do garrison work until he was demobilised in July 1919, surviving the war and thankfully not being added to the names on the Mildenhall Memorial.

Charles Ranns returned to his family in Mildenhall, where he lived out the rest of his life until his death in 1954, at the age of seventy-four years. After his death, his son Charles took over the house on St Andrews Street. Many residents who lived in Mildenhall in the 60s and 70s will remember Charles Ranns (Junior) living in this house and running his shoe shop in a building opposite. The shop was demolished in the 1970s to make way for the shopping precinct which now stands there.

Eliza Graham's oldest daughter Emily, who was fathered by Walter Ranns but took on the name Morley, has so far eluded me in my attempts to discover her life after the workhouse. The last record I can find for her is the census record of 1891, when she was at the old workhouse in the church yard. She is not easy to find with any certainty as she could list her surname as Morley or Ranns (which is often mis-transcribed in records), or she could have married by the time of the 1901 census. Her place of birth was given as Middlesex on the 1881 census but Mildenhall in 1891, so in 1901 she could have listed either. There is also the possibility that she did not make it to 1901 and passed away between census records. I'm sure it's a mystery that can be solved with some further research, so please make contact if you discover any records that might help find her in later years. It would be great to know that she did manage to live a happy life outside the workhouse.

Rosa (Rose) Morley, the first child born to Eliza and Arthur Morley, was born with a disability and on the 1891 census record is listed as an "Imbecile from birth". We cannot know her exact condition but it does seem it was severe enough for her not to be released from the workhouse. In the 1901 census, an 18 year old Rose Morley was still an inmate of the Mildenhall Workhouse, but she was now at the new Kingsway workhouse and is listed as a "lunatic from birth". There was no mental health classification in 1901, and it seems insensitive and ignorant to list household members as either an idiot, imbecile or lunatic.

In the 1911 census record, Rose Morley unsurprisingly continued to be an inmate of the workhouse, again listed next to her aunt Alice Graham, giving us an indication that they were able to look out for each other and have some form of family relationship while living out this nightmare life they had been dealt. Rose was the only remaining child of Eliza in the workhouse, her mental condition now reverted back to "Imbecile from birth". The changing of classification between an Imbecile and Lunatic from one census record to another really does show this to be an unsuitable, poorly considered classification system.

When the army took over the workhouse during the First World War Rose would have transferred to the Newmarket Workhouse along with her aunt. I have no record of her after 1911, so it would be good to know what happened to Rose after the workhouse system was abolished in 1930. Was she transferred to a hospital or asylum? Or was she released to look after herself?

Sarah Morley managed to leave the workhouse at a relatively young age in 1901, and at sixteen years old she was already living and working in London. Sarah had found work as a servant in Wandsworth for John Bland and his son Edward William Bland, who was a clerk for the East India Company. The father of John Bland was Samuel King Bland, a well-known minister and missionary who worked as a kind of un-mitered Bishop around Suffolk. The Suffolk connection seems too much of a coincidence not to be relevant, particularly as the Bland family had owned land in Mildenhall. I do think Sarah Morley was offered a way out of the workhouse by Samuel King Bland and the Board of Guardians, who found work for as many of the workhouse children as they could. Sarah was more than likely placed into work for this family by the Mildenhall Board of Guardians who would have known the Bland family. In 1915, Sarah married John Harvey at St Mary's Mildenhall Church and in 1939 they were living just down the road in Tuddenham.

The youngest surviving son, Arthur Morley, also left the workhouse at a young age. In 1901, at just fourteen years old, Arthur was working as an agricultural labourer in Lakenheath, boarding with a seventy-four year old widow named Elizabeth Brown in the High Street of the same village. Again, it would have been the Board of Guardians that arranged his accommodation and work outside the workhouse.

In 1908 Arthur left England, a country that so far only held bad memories for him. His destination was Canada, a country where he could start afresh, a new life where he could be whatever he wanted and leave the memory of his awful, deprived childhood behind him.

In 1914, Arthur was to start his own family when he married a Canadian by the name of Zelda Desjardine. Together they had three children; all boys, Everett, Milne and Delbert. In 1923, Arthur moved his family to the U.S.A., and they arrived in Seattle in 1923 before moving on to California, where they settled in the small town of Bieber, a beautiful part of America which is surrounded by mountains and lakes.

Arthur had a new, wonderful life surrounded by the love of his new family in what is one of the most beautiful places on our earth, a far cry from his poor days walking around the slum of Fullers' Yard in Mildenhall, starving and poorly clothed on a freezing November evening. However, sadness can occur no matter how beautiful the surroundings, and in 1926 Arthur's wife Zelda passed away, followed by his 15 year old son Delbert in 1933.

Arthur and his son Milne both worked for the Lassen Lumber and

Box Company. Old photos from the lumber mill taken from the time when Arthur would have worked there are amazing. A real life cowboy and western town with landscapes that you instantly recognise from 'spaghetti western' movies. Arthur Graham, the cowboy with the Suffolk accent; I can almost hear him now as he arrives in town and has a look around for the first time *"Cood-a-hell, that's a rum owd dew, oi hint never sin nuth'n loike that afore, hull ut roupe over hear, bor and oi'll tie my hoss up, if oi had a camera or suffen oi'd take a phooter."*

In 1940, Arthur's two surviving sons were drafted into the American Army as part of the Service Act, which required men between the ages of eighteen and forty-five serve the United States in the Second World War. Arthur himself was part of the "old man's draft" which required all men between forty-five to sixty-four to register their skills so that they could be utilised, and younger men could be freed up to fight.

Arthur lived out the rest of his life in the picturesque, postcard perfect area of California, where he died in 1958 in Turlock. Although he did experience the loss of his wife and son, he did manage to make a good life for himself. Out of all the individuals I've researched, it was the children of Eliza Graham that I found most heartbreaking, and it does fill me with some joy to see Arthur take the chance to move to the USA and make a new life. I wonder if he recounted his early life and tales of the workhouse to his sons and grandchildren? I was fortunate to make contact with Arthur's granddaughter in the States who remembered Arthur from when she was a young girl. What really resonates with me is when she told me "Her Pops was the kindest, most loving person she's ever known. His integrity, honesty and humility was well-known and appreciated by all those who knew him". He really did escape the shadow of the workhouse, quite literally the sunshine in the beautiful setting of Lassen County chasing away any shadows of his young life.

CHAPTER FOURTEEN

The Jessups End of an era

The Master and Matron partnership that had been such a success for the past thirty-four years had come to an end. Sarah Jane Jessup, the Workhouse Matron for so many years passed away in April 1913, leaving a broken-hearted Charles to run the workhouse without his wife.

Charles Jessup met with the Board of Guardians and suggested his sister Alice take over as the matron of the workhouse, The Board of Guardians accepted this proposal.

The death of Sarah Jessup was reported with great sadness in the local paper. Sarah balanced perfectly the strict outer demeanor required of the Matron along with compassion and kindness of those in her care, and the generous tributes by the local press were not undeserved: ..."*the esteemed matron of the workhouse*" ..."*very assiduous in her duties*" ..."*always took a kindly interest in those who were under her charge*" ...*her inmates have lost a good friend*" ..."*Mr. and Mrs. Jessup proved admirable officials at the workhouse*" ..."*gained good will and full confidence of the guardians*" ..."*inmates held them in warm regard.*"

Charles worked a further five years as the master of the workhouse, with his sister Alice alongside him as the Matron. In June 1918, they both handed in their resignations and Charles Jessup retired after thirty-nine years as the Master of the Mildenhall workhouse.

The Board of Guardians were not short of applicants to replace them. Forty-two applications were received for the roles of Master and Matron. There was really no need to appoint a new Master or Matron (but they did), as since the outbreak of the First World War, the army had taken over the workhouse building for war work. The inmates of the Mildenhall Workhouse had been transferred to the Newmarket Workhouse and the Mildenhall Workhouse would not open again.

After the death of his wife, Charles Jessup took on some help around his living accommodation in the workhouse and in 1915 employed Florence Cutting, a former workhouse inmate as his servant. She left his service in 1917 but returned a year later to work as a housekeeper for Charles Jessup, who had now retired and lived near Thetford.

Florence Cutting was a controversial choice for Charles to select as an employee. She had given birth to three children in the workhouse, all of which she was accused of abandoning to the workhouse with the Mildenhall Union ratepayers picking up the bill for their upkeep. Florence went on to have a fourth child in 1918. This child was now living with her in Charles Jessup's house, while two of her other children were still being cared for at the expense of the Mildenhall Union, and another had been adopted.

The father of Florence Cutting's first two children was a Mildenhall local named Percy Challis. According to Florence, he had promised to marry her, but while she was in the workhouse he married another woman and was then later killed in the war, (yet again my research brings me to the Mildenhall Memorial).

In October 1920, Florence Cutting was summoned to court, charged with deserting her children. During this trial, Florence Cutting was questioned on several aspects of her personal life. Questions were asked about her relationship with Charles Jessup, and although not asked outright, it was implied that maybe he could be the father of the fourth child. This line of questioning was soon shut down by her representation. It was highly controversial for Charles to have allowed himself to be so closely associated with a former young inmate, especially an inmate who was viewed as abusing the system by abandoning her children. The below extracts from the trial come from the Lynn Advertiser on 16th October 1920:

A social problem of a very distressing nature was revealed at the Mildenhall

Sessions ..Florence Cutting ...appeared before Major-General Lindley, Mr. Favor Parker and Dr A.J. Pickworth on an adjourned charge of deserting two children so that they became chargeable to the Common fund of Mildenhall Union ...L. Dighton appeared for the Guardians and Mr H Bankes Ashton for the woman.

The charge was under the Poor Law Amendment act of 1884, which provided that a woman deserting her bastard child whereby it became chargeable to the Common Fund could be punished as a rogue and vagabond, the punishment was six calendar months' hard labour...

In July 1909 defendant went into Mildenhall Workhouse and gave birth to a boy, Cyril Jack, who from that time until now had been chargeable to the Union. In 1911 she returned to the Workhouse and gave birth to another child, Stanley Dennis, who was also chargeable to the Guardians. In 1913 again in the Workhouse, another child was born, Annie Phyllis, this girl being boarded out by the Guardians ...and subsequently adopted ...and now not a charge on the Union...

Mr Dighton said that the woman took her discharge from the Workhouse in 1915 and went into employ of the master (C. Jessup) as a domestic servant. She left that employ in 1917 and went to London. When she returned to the district she again entered the employ of the Master, who at that time had retired ...she was now in his employment as housekeeper.

She had been requested on several occasions to remove the children and provide accommodation for them ...she had written declining that was why she was charged ...The boy Cyril was now boarded out at the Newmarket Workhouse and the other boy in Mildenhall.

She wrote a letter that she was not in a position to maintain the two children "which the Mildenhall Guardians took from me," that three years ago she was ordered by the Guardians to leave the Workhouse where she was employed and that the Guardians took her children and put them with other people without her being consulted.

Mr Banks Ashton called the defendant who said the same man was the father of the first two children...He promised to marry her but while she was in the workhouse married another woman. He was later killed in the war... She was now assisting Mr. Jessup, formerly the Workhouse Master, and now a greengrocer and florist. He paid her 10s weekly and provided lodging and she had to find part of her board, buy her clothes and keep another child out of her 10s...

Mr Dighton's first question in cross examination "Are you married to Mr. Jessup? A question to which witness replied in the negative. Mr. Dighton proceeded to question the witness as to the fourth child, which she said was two

years old, she claimed the father of this child was killed in the war. Mr. Ashton
strongly objected to any questions in regard to any of the children except the two
mentioned in the summons......Mr. Ashton said that the woman has said on oath
that the father had been killed in action, and the statement must be accepted. It was
unfair to harass this poor creature who had lost the man responsible...

Mr Dighton: Do you say that out of your 10s. you have to find your own
board? Witness, Yes...- Do you suggest that Mr. Jessup only pays you £26 a
year, takes your services and makes you find for yourself and baby out of 10s a
week? Do you ask the Bench to believe that any man can be so inhumane as to
engage a servant and pay her the magnificent sum of £26 and expect her to do all
the work and find her own food? I have to do so. - Can you not find work
elsewhere? I have not tried. - As a matter of fact you are married, are you not? -
Defendant: No, I am not- Mr. Ashton (to Mr Dighton) All your instructions are
wrong.

Mr Bankes Ashton said he was sorry if he had shown undue warmth, but
when a man was attacked in his absence he thought it was not unusual for an
advocate to stand up for him.

Without question, this entire situation and court case would have
cast a bad light on Charles Jessup in the eyes of some locals and
prompted questions regarding his time as the Master of the
Workhouse.

In 1924, eleven years after the death of his wife Sarah Jane, the
seventy year old Charles Jessup remarried. His new wife was thirty-
seven years younger than him, and was just thirty-three years old.
His new wife was Florence Cutting! Maybe Charles had married for
the convenience of having had a wife to care for him in his later years,
a mutually beneficial arrangement where Charles was able to provide
financially for Florence. Maybe Charles was the father of her fourth
child, or maybe the couple had just fallen in love during the time
Florence was working for the former workhouse master!

Charles had moved away from Mildenhall, which was probably
for the best, as I am sure that if he had stayed in the town, he would
have been the subject of much gossip. Charles moved just fifteen miles
up the road to Santon Downham, where Florence Cutting and her
youngest child joined him, Florence as an employee and boarder
before becoming his wife.

In 1930 one of the boys, Stanley Cutting, whom Florence had left
behind in the workhouse, died after an accident on the river Little

Ouse at the Brandon Staunch. The newspaper report, in addition to detailing the tragic accident, also informs us that Stanley and Cyril were now living with Charles Jessup, Florence and her youngest child. What a sad end to the life of Stanley Cutting. His father had died in the war, his mother had little option but to abandon him to the workhouse, and reunited with his family he had died at the age of twenty.

Stanley Cutting had gone to Brandon Staunch, along with his two brothers, to bathe one Sunday afternoon. Stanley changed into his bathing costume before climbing the fifteen feet high diving board from which he dived, hitting the water with his stomach and becoming winded. Three other men who were at the same spot bathing that day dived in to rescue him, and after great difficulty they managed to rescue him onto a passing boat. The men "applied artificial respiration" for some considerable time until Stanley Cutting could breathe more easily. Stanley was then dressed and helped onto a boat, which then took him to the Ouse Hotel where he got a car home. Two days later Stanley died at the Jessup household. The mourners at his funeral included Mrs. Jessup (Mother), Mr. Jessup, Master Charles Cutting, Master R. Jessup (Brothers). Interestingly the list of mourners shows that Florence's youngest child was now using the name Jessup!

After an eventful life and over forty years working in four different workhouses for three different unions, I would have thought Charles Jessup would want to peacefully retire in this rural setting. However, in February 1926, Charles again found himself in court. This had been a regular occurrence over the years, although since his jewellery theft as a young seventeen year old he had only been summoned in court to give evidence against paupers and inmates of his workhouse. Now at the age of seventy-two, he found himself back in court as the defendant.

Charles was accused of poaching at Croxton (a small village near Thetford) and killing game without a licence. The game keeper, Harry Eagle, had heard a gunshot at 2:30am and along with a friend, Walter Stearn, he went to investigate. On their way towards the gunshot they heard another ten shots.

Harry Eagle flashed his torch towards Charles Jessup. Charles' accomplice for the night, Thomas Davey, was seen carrying a sack.

Davey dropped the sack and ran away, leaving an elderly Charles alone with the gamekeepers. Harry Eagle struck Charles Jessup with a cane at which point he fell to the floor, but immediately jumped up to grab Eagle by the throat. Charles may have been an old man but he obviously still had some fight left in him. There was a terrible struggle, both men being injured before Eagle called out for help from his friend, Walter Stearn.

Stearn managed to release Charles' hands from the gamekeeper's throat and at this point Charles Jessup suffered severe injuries, although the gamekeeper and his friend deny beating him or hitting him while he was down.

Eagle and Stearn left Charles Jessup laying on the floor and went for a drink of brandy at the Bell public house, The two men deny leaving the scene believing Charles Jessup to be dead. When the men finished their brandy, they returned to deal with Charles but they found his body had disappeared and fled the scene.

Covered in blood and seriously wounded, Charles Jessup made it to his house where he was then bedridden for seven weeks, resulting in his trial for poaching being postponed. As a seventeen year old, Charles had come up with a very unlikely story to cover his crime, and now at the age of seventy-two, Charles had a story to defend himself that sounds just as unlikely. Charles Jessup said, in his defence, that he felt he had invented a way to silence a gun and was so obsessed with the idea that he went out with the poacher that night to see how well it worked. Charles had seven weeks in bed to formulate his defence and this was the best with which he could come up. If this was somehow true it was clearly a flawed invention, as the gamekeepers heard it go off eleven times! Charles Jessup was given a fine of £10 a month for six months as well as a fine of £3 for killing game without a license.

Since his arrival in Mildenhall, Charles had been a regular name in the local papers, mainly due to his role as Master of the Workhouse. He also appeared as an award winning florist, and as part of the Mildenhall Town Football Team and the Mildenhall Volunteer Rifles. His final and last appearance was in 1934 when his death was announced at the age of seventy-eight.

Charles Jessup certainly packed a lot into his seventy-eight years, a man who would have been instantly recognisable and known to all of Mildenhall in his time, now almost wiped from history, swept under the carpet and hidden away, along with the history of the workhouses.

CHAPTER FIFTEEN

Mildenhall Workhouse removing the shadow 1915 to 1960

In July 1915, the Mildenhall Board of Guardians received a letter from the local government board informing them of a request from the British Army to use the workhouse as a military hospital for the duration of the war. The Mildenhall Board of Guardians wrote letters to neighbouring local Poor Unions to inquire about the possibility of the Mildenhall inmates being accommodated at their workhouse in the event the army took over the Mildenhall building. Thetford confirmed they could help with the request, but they could only take fifty inmates and this was only if they were not infirmary patients. The army did not act upon their request and for the time being the Mildenhall inmates remained housed at the Kingsway site.

Life was obviously very far from normal for the inmates during the war years. Along with the rest of the country, they were required to adhere to the blackout restrictions. This blackout order, which had now become nationwide having initially only been imposed on coastal towns, was an attempt to reduce the success of German Zeppelin raids. Neighbouring towns to Mildenhall had already been targeted by the German Zeppelins. Great Yarmouth, Kings Lynn, Bury St Edmunds, Newmarket and Ipswich all had been bombed. This was a terrifying new type of warfare that brought the horror of war to the doorstep of the British public.

My own family had experienced the terror of these raids. My great-great-uncle John Pearson was the landlord of the Anchor Public

House in Northgate Street, Bury St. Edmunds at the time the war had started. One night in April 1916, while he was sleeping in his bedroom upstairs in the pub, the unoccupied bedroom next to him was caved in by a bomb that had been dropped by a Zeppelin airship. The Anchor Public House received too much damage to be saved, and was demolished following the bombing. Amazingly, no lives were lost, and even more remarkably, John Pearson did not wake from his sleep until the police disturbed him to check that he was all right.

On 25th November 1916, Charles Jessup, the Master of the Workhouse, found himself in breach of the blackout. At 6p.m. Superintendent Heigham was walking down Kingsway, when he observed lights coming from the workhouse. Bright lights were beaming out from the skylight over the kitchen, the windows of the dining hall and the glass roof in the scullery. When Superintendent Heigham knocked on the door, Charles Jessup took him into the workshop, a large room which was lit by candle; into the dining hall, where there was one incandescent burner on and into the scullery where there was a gas jet turned down. Charles Jessup was summoned to appear in court to answer charges of breaching the lights order. It was decided that there had been too much light coming from the workhouse, and particularly the light from the skylight was remarked upon as being very dangerous. Charles Jessup was fined £1. Mr. Jessup in his defence submitted that *"the structural arrangement of the workhouse was such that it was impossible to conduct it without light. There were more than 300 windows, besides skylights and glass corridors."*

Charles Jessup's description of the glass incorporated into the design of the workhouse and the vast number of windows certainly illustrates what a grand mansion this Victorian building was.

In April 1918, the British army finally followed through on their request to take over the Mildenhall Workhouse. It was repurposed as a hospital for wounded soldiers and run by the army. The Mildenhall inmates were transferred to the Newmarket Workhouse, although it was agreed that Newmarket would not take any "bed ridden" inmates or "mental cases". Presumably these individuals must have been located at local asylums and hospitals.

In December 1918 at the Newmarket Board of Guardians meeting, it was discussed that six of the former Mildenhall inmates were "certified imbeciles" and that their case papers should be sent to the

Newmarket Guardians. It was requested that they be re-certified. It is very likely that Rose Morley and Alice Graham were two of the six "imbeciles" received from Mildenhall.

After the war, the Mildenhall inmates who had not already left by their own means remained at the Newmarket Workhouse. The numbers had dwindled from the one hundred and thirty inmates of Mildenhall Union in 1900 to around thirty-five by the end of the war. Following the war, Mildenhall Workhouse never opened its doors again as a fully functioning workhouse. The much celebrated end of the war had marked the beginning of the end for workhouses across Britain.

The Poor Law System had been declining since the end of the nineteenth century, as it was no longer a suitable solution for dealing with the poor. Attitudes were changing, and it was clear that locking the poorer members of society in a building together was not the best way forward. Other forms of assistance had slowly been supplementing the Poor Law system, which meant that the poor were less reliant on the in-house relief offered by the poor Unions.

Friendly societies were formed and grew in popularity. These societies allowed local people and neighbours, often with a shared interest, to form a club and pay a small sum of money each month into a shared pot. In times of need, such as a funeral, unemployment and even death of an animal, members were paid money out of this collective pot. There were many of these societies and one of the best known society in the local area to Mildenhall was the Ancient Shepherds Benefit Society

In 1886, the Chamberlain Circular was issued, which encouraged the setting up of work relief projects in times of high unemployment and was a clear indication that the government was moving away from the poor law system. In 1905, another scheme, the Unemployed Workman Act, offered grants to businesses to allow them to hire unemployed workers. However, workers with a criminal background were excluded from this scheme.

The "Old Age Pension" was introduced in 1909 and many of the inmates who were too old or infirm to work could now survive outside the workhouse on the pension. This greatly reduced the population of inmates across the country. The National Insurance Scheme was introduced in 1911, and the employee, employer and government all paid in for each employee. The system was very manual and employees would have to buy stamps which were affixed to the National Insurance Card. When the employment ended the employee was *"given his cards"*, and these cards were the proof of any benefits to which the employee was entitled during hard times, such as illness, maternity cover, or medical care.

Despite the slow erosion of the Poor Law Act since the end of the previous century, it was the poverty of the inter-war years that killed off the workhouse system. The Board of Guardians Act of 1926 allowed the government to replace the Guardians with government officials if they felt it was required. This was very much a reaction to Boards of Guardians supporting the miners in the strikes of 1926.

After the First World War, there was an increase of people who required aid from the poor law system, and many of these people were offered outdoor relief. In 1921 George Lansbury, a leader of the Labour Party, had led rebellions against the poor law rates, which were higher in areas with larger concentrations of poverty. Lansbury had previously issued a pamphlet in 1911 entitled *"Smash up the Workhouse!"*

The Local Government Act of 1929 was the final nail in the coffin of the Poor Law Unions. Any remaining Boards of Guardians were abolished, including the Mildenhall Board. Local authorities took over workhouses, and they were rebranded "as public assistance institutions".

In June 1919, the Mildenhall Board of Guardians discussed the damage caused by the military during its occupation of the Kingsway site. The valuers of the Board and the War Department put the cost of repairs at £253 and 6s. Aware of the changing landscape regarding the poor law, the Board of Guardians asked the clerk to write to H.M. Inspectorate to ascertain if the Guardians' functions were likely to be superseded by new legislation before carrying out any renovation, or giving notice to terminate the arrangement with the Newmarket union.

In February 1920, at the monthly Mildenhall Board of Guardians meeting, a contract was agreed between the Mildenhall Union and Newmarket Union to house the Mildenhall inmates (now just thirty-two people) at Newmarket for a cost of 17s 6d per head per week, with twelve months' notice to be given by either side to terminate the agreement. Mrs. Fanny Marshall, who lived in the last thatched house in Mildenhall (now the site of the dentist), was a member of the Mildenhall Guardians. She was quite persistent in her arguments that the Mildenhall inmates should return to the Kingsway site so that they could be closer to their families, and felt that the cost of housing inmates could be offset by growing vegetables in the grounds of the Workhouse. She also had strong opinions that the workhouse should not be left to rot and decay, but she was somewhat of a lone voice and in a minority with this opinion amongst the Guardians.

Odden Fredric Read (Chairman of the Board of Guardians) stated:

"When the house was built 30 years ago, things were entirely different, there was no old age pension and the workhouse was the only alternative that old people had. Now circumstances have altered and they have a pension, there was less application for indoor relief". He put it to the board that you cannot run the institution for the sake of a few paupers. "No doubt they would like to see their friends but the Guardians must not be ruled by sentiment". Odden Fredric Read went on to state "It is not expedient at the present time to take any steps for the reopening of the workhouse, they would make a good deal of money letting the building" Another member of the board said "everything was being done to reduce pauperism, the time will come when there would be no need for the workhouses (hear hear)".

After much debate a majority vote eventually decided that the inmates should remain in Newmarket, and discussions soon turned then turned to what should be done with the disused workhouse building. The clerk read a letter from the Ministry of Health stating that *"the Ministry were prepared to give favourable consideration to a proposal for the accommodation of mental defectives".* Chairmen Odden Fredric Read suggested that they advertise the workhouse for let in the local newspapers and they should not bind themselves to accept any tender. It was agreed to write a letter to the Ministry of Health informing them of their intentions.

The Guardians received interest from Cambridge County Council and the Church of the Universal Bond, but offers were either not followed up or not deemed acceptable. The Board of Guardians were discovering it is not easy to offload such a large building, and they struggled to let or sell the workhouse. They had several inquiries for purchasing the workhouse, or at least parts of it. The Hammersmith Board of Guardians had inquired about the laundry plant on the

Mildenhall site, while another letter they received from the County Surveyor requested the purchase of any granite they might have. It was agreed to sell both broken and unbroken granite to the surveyor.

In July 1920, the Board of Guardians wrote to the Newmarket Board of Guardians to inform them that they were preparing to sell the furniture from the Mildenhall Workhouse. The letter listed the items that they thought the Newmarket Union might be interested in purchasing. It now seemed very unlikely the Mildenhall Workhouse would ever open as a workhouse again. Newmarket agreed to a price of £300 for a large amount of the furniture and also some clothing. In October of the same year, Mildenhall again wrote to Newmarket informing them that although they had invoiced them £300, the value of the furniture had since increased and they would need to pay £360. This strange increase that the Mildenhall Board tried to spring on Newmarket was not accepted and the furniture and clothing was sold for £300.

In his book, "160 Years of Service to the Community: History of Newmarket General Hospital", Dick Heasman, whose family for many years worked at the Newmarket Workhouse, recalls seeing as late as 1947 large meat dishes with "Mildenhall Workhouse" marked in the centre of the dish. These dishes would have been part of the purchase of items in 1920. A Mildenhall Workhouse dinner plate can also be seen on display at the Mildenhall museum, a very large heavy plate printed with the words "Mildenhall Workhouse" and a date of "1909".

The Mildenhall Union residents remained boarded at Newmarket, but Mildenhall continued operating its casual ward for vagrant paupers. In October 1920, this ward was also closed, at which point Mr. Francis E. Bloss (Mildenhall Union clerk) wrote to the Newmarket Board of Guardians. His letter informed the Newmarket Guardians that the Workhouse in Mildenhall would be closing along with the vagrants' ward, and asked that a letter be placed in the Newmarket Casual wards to inform any vagrants present that they would not be able to travel on to Mildenhall to find accommodation. This letter did not please the Newmarket Guardians, and the Vice chairman voiced his opinion:

"The closing of the Mildenhall casual ward would throw the casuals into other Unions' Workhouses, there is a certain amount of casuals and they must go somewhere. If we put this notice up in the Newmarket casual ward, we would

have more tramps coming here than before. Mildenhall was not doing its fair share in the matter. In Cambridgeshire there was a very fair and equitable system of pooling the cost of the casual relief so Unions with casual wards and those without casual wards would pay the same. But there is no such system in Suffolk."

Mrs. Fanny Marshall died in December 1920, and along with her died the lone voice on the Board of Guardians that the workhouse should reopen. The Guardians, unable to find a buyer of the site, decided they should employ a caretaker to look after the building. Perhaps Mrs. Marshall's views that the building should not fall into disrepair were being listened to posthumously. The vacancy for caretaker was posted in the Bury Free Press on New Year's Day 1921.

THE MILDENHALL BOARD OF GUARDIANS

require a **CARETAKER AND WIFE** *for their institution, which is unoccupied.*

The persons appointed will have to look after the garden and land adjoining and to keep the House aired and clean.

Unfurnished rooms will be provided by the Guardians.

Apply, stating age, wages required, and with copies of two recent testimonials to be sent to me by the 6th day of January, 1921.

FRANCIS E BLOSS

Clerk to the Guardians, Mildenhall, Suffolk

This advertisement, which describes unfurnished rooms, really demonstrates that the Board of Guardians were selling everything they could possibly sell to claw back money spent on the workhouse over the years and reduce the ongoing burden on the local ratepayers.

The Bury Free Press carried an advertisement in the Auctioneers announcements on 15th January 1921. The Mildenhall Board of Guardians was selling off any remaining items that it had been unable to offload to the Newmarket Union.

SHORT NOTICE SALE.

Kingsway, **MILDENHALL**

Messrs. BELL & BILSLAND

HAVE been favoured with instructions from Mildenhall Board of Guardians to sell by auction (from a written catalogue),

at the Workhouse, Kingsway, on FRIDAY, Jan. 21st, 1921, at 11 a.m. prompt,

a quantity of **HOUSEHOLD FURNITURE**

Including 30 Iron Bedsteads, Tables, Cupboards, Overmantles, Meat Safes,

Standup Writing Desk with Cupboard and Brass Rack, Stationery Case and numerous other effects, also a quantity of Outdoor Implements, including 16 Iron Circular Pig Troughs, 2 cross cut saws etc., etc.

The auction brought in £52 9s 9d, and this, together with the sale of furniture and items to Newmarket meant that the Guardians had recovered £352 9s 9d, worth in the region of £17,000 today.

The local ratepayers had become increasingly frustrated with seeing the large building sit empty on the edge of their town. They had contributed taxes towards the large cost of this building just twenty-five years earlier, and were not happy about the situation. Letters written to the local papers were frequent, and debate about the workhouse was a hot topic around the streets of Mildenhall. The letter below was printed by the Bury Free Press in February 1921.

Mildenhall Empty Workhouse
To the editor of "the Bury Free Press"

Sir, I notice attention is again called to our "white elephant" — the unoccupied Mildenhall workhouse, described as a "Mansion standing in its freehold acres". It seems to me about time we ratepayers had a voice in the matter. This fine building has been standing empty for two years, and although we gather from the Press that various negotiations have taken place with a view to letting, the report generally concludes "it was adjourned to the next Board meeting" and there the matter apparently ends. I fail to see what better use the buildings could be put than that for which they were designed, for I have heard them spoken of as a "model workhouse" and after all the thousands of pounds of ratepayers' money which have been poured out, it seems little short of a scandal to have the placed closed, and all the money previously spent in the town sent to Newmarket. Why was not the offer of the Thetford Union to come here not accepted and so allow us to bring our own people back from Newmarket? I have repeatedly heard it said that "he who pays the piper should call the tune", and I certainly think that such an important question should have been decided by the whole of the ratepayers of the Union, and not left to ten or a dozen men, however capable they may be, who were not elected on the Board to decide whether or not the inmates should be permanently removed, and the place closed. One more point; it hardly seemed necessary to retain the services of the Master and Matron and a stoker for two and a half years. Perhaps there is some satisfactory explanation, but from the meagre Press reports, the poor ratepayers are left in the dark. I may say I am only re-echoing the opinions I have frequently heard expressed throughout the district.

Yours truly ,

ONE OF THE POOR RATEPAYERS.
Mildenhall.

Another year passed, and in January 1922 the Board of Guardians were still struggling to offload their giant white elephant. At the monthly Board meeting, a letter was read from a Mr. D. Luker, who had been tasked with finding a buyer. His letter, reporting back to the Board of Guardians, said that he had been unable to obtain any proposal he could lay before them as to the disposal of the Mildenhall Workhouse. Mr. Luker had forwarded to seven London institutions the particulars of the Mildenhall Workhouse, but no replies were received.

In March 1923, after another year of unsuccessful attempts to sell the workhouse, the Mildenhall Board of Guardians wrote to the Ministry of Health, suggesting that the disused workhouse be used as a sanatorium (a medical facility set up for treatment of tuberculosis) for Suffolk. The letter was sent on to the tuberculosis sub-committee who were at the time setting up a sanatorium in Suffolk, but the Board of Guardians was not taken up on its offer. In July 1923, the Guardians requested that the district valuer write a report for them detailing the value of the workhouse, with a view to selling the building through Messer, Knight, Frank and Rutley of Hanover Street, London.

In April 1924, the Workhouse was finally sold! Auctioneers Knight, Frank and Rutley sold the site at auction in the Angel Hotel, Bury St Edmunds, for a sum of £2,550. It had been purchased by an Ipswich firm of housebreakers who set about breaking down the buildings. The materials, now more valuable than when the building was erected, were being carted away piecemeal for use in other places. I have seen photos of the breaking taking place (which can be seen on this book's Facebook page), and even now nearly one hundred years later it is painful to view such an expensive and magnificent Victorian construction being demolished. It would have stood as a very attractive building in the town today, had the guardians managed to sell it to a buyer who had a use for a building rather than selling it off piece by piece as building materials. It would have been at this time that Odden Read rescued the foundation stone he had previously laid in 1895, the same stone that I discovered earlier this year (2021) in the wall of Odden Read's former residence.

In the Mildenhall Almanack and Directory of 1925, a comment

regarding the demolition of the workhouse was made: *"The ruins of a formerly handsome building in the Kingsway, Mildenhall, are not pleasant to look upon ...In the opinion of many it was a great mistake that the institution was ever closed down as a workhouse and probably the Board if they could have seen the ultimate result would have hesitated in taking that decision."*

After the breaking down and selling of most of the building, a central portion of the workhouse remained along with a flint cottage. The site and remaining structures were then sold in July 1925 to Albert Elijah White, who lived in the remaining part of the building and used the land as a poultry and pig farm.

The workhouse system was nearing the end, and in 1929 the Local Government Act made changes to the Poor Law, which included abolishing the Poor Law Unions and their Board of Guardians. Their powers were transferred to the local county councils. Workhouses were rebranded as public assistance institutions, but very little changed in the quality of accommodation, and the institutions were still more often than not referred to as "workhouses".

In March 1930, the Mildenhall Union Board of Guardians met for their last ever meeting, the Board having been abolished by the 1929 Act. At the conclusion of business, the chairman Mr. Odden Read gave a speech: *"I very greatly regret that this will be the last meeting of the board I will preside over, I have been a member for close upon 50 years and chairman of the board for 40 years. I feel personally the passing very much. No one here, except myself, attended the meetings of the board in Church Lane. I had the honour of laying the foundation stone of the workhouse on Kingsway and I have the same stone now in my garden, which was taken out when the workhouse was sold and pulled down, rather unique, I think you'll agree. As to the future, I am afraid that personal touch, which is so essential to the administration of the work of the Guardians will be lost and the poor will not be looked after so well as they have been under the old regime, I really think we should follow other boards and have a photograph taken".*

The Workhouses, or "public assistance institutions"as they were now officially known, finally came to an end in 1948 when the National Health Service (N.H.S.) came into force. The control of the remaining institutions was transferred from county councils to the newly formed N.H.S. and they became hospitals or retirement homes. Many hospitals still had casual wards for vagrants right up to the 1960s.

In 1949, a local Mildenhall family bought the former workhouse site in Kingsway and lived there until 1960, when the remaining central block was finally cleared to make way for the new police station, library and council offices. It is often written that the workhouse was demolished in 1924. When local historian Dr. Colin Dring released his brilliant book "Around Mildenhall in Old Photographs" he too made reference to the demolition beginning in 1924. This prompted the lady who had bought the property in 1949 to write to Dr Dring. The letter she wrote is kept on file in one of the back rooms at Mildenhall Museum, who were kind enough to let me read it.

In the letter she informs Dr Dring that, together with her husband, they had bought the workhouse in 1949 and lived there until they had to move out so that the new police station could be built. In the letter she writes that she fought hard for two years to save what was left of the workhouse and to keep her home until a sale was forced upon them. The letter gives a clue that there was at least one out building left at the time, as the lady informs Dr Dring that she and her husband used to make wreaths in the laundry block which was at the back of the house. The letter ends stating that she has the original documents of the house and many photos which might be of interest. I'm not sure if Dr Dring ever got to see these documents or received copies of them, but they would be of great interest to me and I would love to see them. I have trawled through the files available at Mildenhall Museum and they are not in file, where the lady's letter is kept.

Fast forward to present day 2021 and a new "Mildenhall Hub" has just been officially opened which brings many public services, Leisure Centre, swimming pool and the Secondary school all onto one site. This new building is colossal in size with its state-of-the-art facilities, and it will be a tremendous asset to the people of Mildenhall. It is not a project that was warmly welcomed by all the residents and caused much debate about the need for such a large structure on the outskirts of the town, built on farmland. These debates are mirrored in history and are the exact same debates and conversations that filled the town when the Kingsway Workhouse was built in 1895.

Ironically, there will now be a new debate over the Mildenhall Kingsway Workhouse site, with the police station, Library, gym and council offices all relocating to the new Hub, and yet again the site that stood empty from 1920 to 1924 is empty again. Now causing debates, discussions and rumours again as Mildenhall residents discuss the best use for this site. In our modern society we now have these debates on social media rather than in the press, but no doubt the debate remains the same. What will happen to this now empty site, which once cast its shadow over the town of Mildenhall and the lives of its most destitute and desperate residents?

Sources

Books
Heasman. D & Melleney. J. R (1996) *160 Years of Service to the Community: History of Newmarket General Hospital.* Mid Anglia Community Health NHS Trust

Higginbotham. P (2014) *The Workhouse Encyclopedia* The History Press

Archer. I & Coe. W. (1994) *Two East Anglian Diaries* Boydell Press: Suffolk Records Society

Beeton. I (1861) *Mrs. Beeton's Book of Household Management* Ward, Lock & Co.

Gifford. J (1829) *English Lawyer or Every Man his own Lawyer* A Whellier, London

Simpson, A. E. (1901) *A History of Mildenhall and its celebrities of the past* S.R. Simpson, Mildenhall

Dring C. M. (1996) *Mildenhall in Old Picture Postcards* European Library

Dring C. M. (1994) Around Mildenhall In Old Photographs Alan Sutton Publishing Limited

Websites
British Newspaper Archive *www.britishnewspaperarchive.co.uk*

Ancestry *www.ancestry.co.uk*

Ancestorian *www.ancestorian.com*

Famous Fights of Past and Present *archive.org/stream/famousfights1/famousfights1_djvu.txt*

Fold 3 military Records *www.fold3.com*

Undying Memory Mildenhall War memorial *www.undyingmemory.net/Mildenhall*

General Records Office *www.gro.gov.uk*

Records
Mildenhall Museum
Ipswich Record Office
Parish Records

Thank You

You have reached the end of my book, I honestly hope you have enjoyed the read and learnt something about the Town of Mildenhall and the Workhouse system.

Reviews are everything for anyone that self publishes, if you have 5 minutes to spare please do go to Amazon and leave a review for this book, it would mean everything for me to be able to share my book with more people, website algorithms make this very difficult to achieve organically without a constant growing list of reviews on their site.

So if you enjoyed this please let me know via the Amazon review function and do come and join us on the books Facebook page .

If you visit my website (suffolkhistorybooks.com) or Facebook page please do subscribe to the newsletter if you'd like to hear about future projects

Thank You

Danny

Mildenhall Market Cross, circa 1900

Mildenhall High Street, circa 1900

Drawing of Mildenhall Church, by Thomas Lyus, 1787

Mildenhall Market Place, circa 1890

The Old Parish Workhouse as it is today in 2021

The Master and Matron accommodation located at the old Parish Workhouse

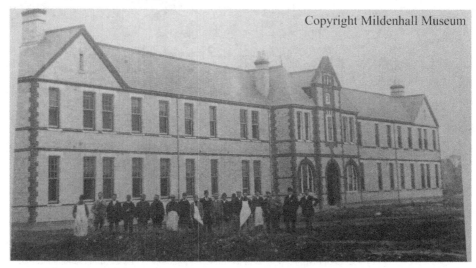

The New Workhouse, shortly after it's construction in 1895

The New Workhouse, several years after it's construction. The detailed stonework now covered in ivy

The Henry Saxon Snell 1886 deisgn. This workhouse was deisgned for a site in St Andrews Street but was never built

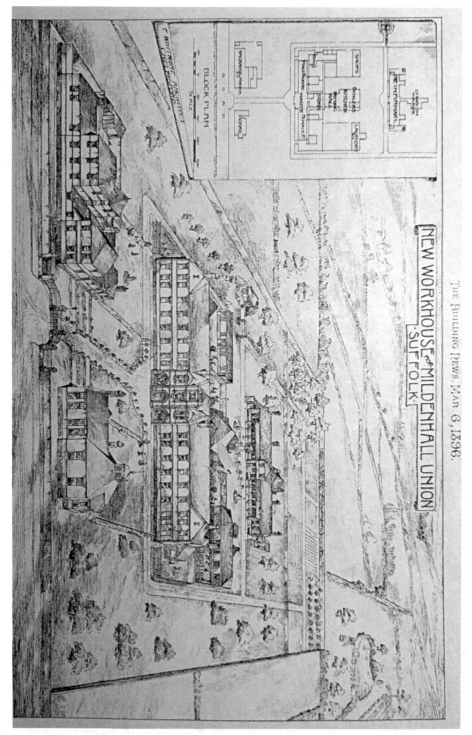

The new Workhouse built in Kingsway in 1895

"The Limes" as it is today in 2021 and inset Odden Read

Number 4 Church Walk. Odden Read's business premises.
Wills were discovered in the loft here in the late 1990s .

Left photo: The Limes sign, rotting away "on the huh"

Right photo: The sign restored, my small memorial to Odden Read

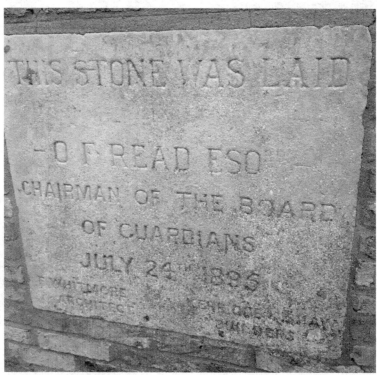

The 1895 Workhouse foundation stone,
as it sits today in the wall outside "The Limes"

Mildenhall War Memorial being Unveiled in 1920

Mildenhall War Memorial in the late 1920s

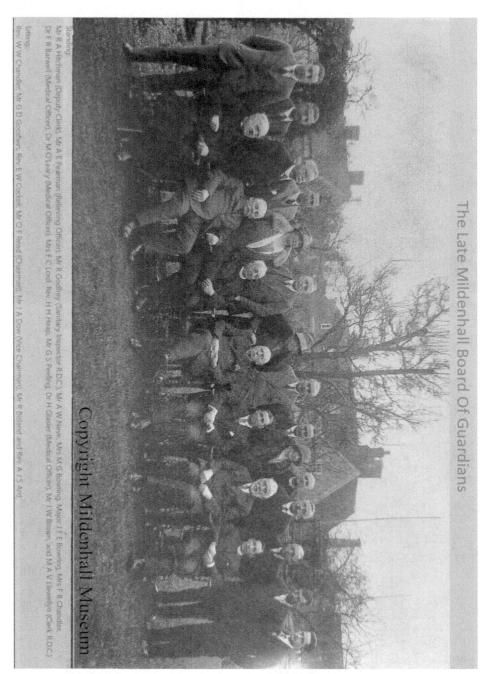

The Late Mildenhall Board Of Guardians

Standing:
Mr R A Hitchman (Deputy Clerk), Mr A E Pearman (Relieving Officer), Mr R Godfrey (Sanitary Inspector R.D.C.), Mr A W Neve, Mrs M G Bowring, Major J F E Bowring, Mrs F B Chandler,
Dr F R Barwell (Medical Officer), Dr M O'Leary (Medical Officer), Mrs F C Lord, Rev. H H Heap, Mr G S Peeling, Dr H Glasser (Medical Officer), Mr J W Brown, and M A V Llewellyn (Clerk R.D.C.)

Sitting:
Rev. W W Chandler, Mr G D Goodwin, Rev. E W Cockett, Mr O F Read (Chairman), Mr J A Dow (Vice Chairman), Mr R Bisland and Rev. A J S Ard.

The Mildenhall Union Board of Guardians, after their last ever meeting

A Workhouse dinnerplate, on display in Mildenhall Museum

The Kingsway Workhouse being demolished in the 1920s